SYNTHESIS

An Introduction to the History, Theory, & Practice of Electronic Music

Alfred PUBLISHERS

ALFRED PUBLISHING CO., INC., NEW YORK

SYNTHESIS

An Introduction to the History, Theory, & Practice of Electronic Music

Herbert A. Deutsch

Hofstra University

Published by Alfred Publishing Co., Inc.
75 Channel Drive, Port Washington, N.Y. 11050

Copyright © 1976 by Alfred Publishing Co., Inc.
All Rights Reserved.

Printed in the United States of America

Library of Congress Cataloging in Publication Data

Deutsch, Herbert A
   Synthesis: an introduction to the history, theory
and practice of electronic music.

   Bibliography: p.
   1. Electronic music–History and criticism.
2. Electronic music–Instruction and study. I. Title
ML3817.D5   789.9   76-20709
ISBN 0-88284-043-6 pbk

I long for instruments obedient to my thought and which, with their contribution of a whole new world of unsuspected sounds, will lend themselves to the exigencies of my inner rhythm.

Edgard Varèse, 1917

We also have sound-houses, where we practise and demonstrate all sounds, and their generation. We have harmonies which you have not, of quarter sounds and lesser slides of sounds. Diverse Instruments of Musick likewise to you unknowne, some sweeter than you have; together with Bells and Rings that are dainty and sweet. We represent small sounds as well as Great and Deepe.... We make diverse Tremblings and Warblings of sounds.... We have certain helps, which set to the ears doe further hearing greatly. We have strange and artificial echos, reflecting the voice many times, as if it were tossing it.... We have also means to convey sounds in trunks and pipes, in strange lines and distances ....

Roger Bacon
"The New Atlantis" 1624

ACKNOWLEDGMENTS

The author wishes to acknowledge the following persons, without whom this book could never have been written:

His wife Peggy, whose support, criticism and honest evaluations of his work have been the most valuable guide to his own awareness of himself as a performer, composer and teacher.

His friend and colleague, Professor Albert Tepper of Hofstra University who, as his teacher, introduced him to electronic music.

Hofstra University Professors Sterling Gorrill and Herman Burstein for their assistance and suggestions.

Geoffrey Feldman, for information on the SYNTHI digital sequencer.

Finally, to Robert Moog, with whom, in a hot July in 1964, a world opened.

CONTENTS

Preface   *xi*

CHAPTER 1: TODAY'S MUSICAL VOCABULARY

Impressionism: The Discovery of Sound as Color   3
Serialism and Atonality: Organization v. Inspiration   4
Dadaism: The Breakdown of the "Logical" in Art   7
Silence and Sonority: A Redefinition of Musical Time   9
Aleatory and Improvisation: Theories of Chance
   and Indeterminacy   12
Conclusion — Eclecticism: The Whole is Greater
   Than Its Parts   15

CHAPTER 2: A SHORT HISTORY OF ELECTRONIC MUSIC

Developments Before World War II   19
The Tape Recorder And Musique Concrète   24
Modern Electronic Music, Phase I   26
Modern Electronic Music, Phase II   28
1963–1965, A Personal Recollection   29
Modern Electronic Music, Phase III   31

CHAPTER 3: THE TAPE RECORDER AS A MUSICAL INSTRUMENT

Recording Tape   38
Tape-Head Configuration   39

Tape Reversal 41
Tape-Speed Variations 42
Splicing 44
Tape Loops 45
Sound-On-Sound 46
Signal-to-Noise Ratio 48
Tape-Head Echo 50
Tape Studio Setup 52
Spatial Sound "Location" 54
Microphones 55

CHAPTER 4: THE ELECTRONIC SYNTHESIS OF SOUND

Basics 56
The Loudspeaker 63
Oscillators and Waveforms 64
Amplifiers 68

PHOTOGRAPHS

CHAPTER 5: ELECTRONIC MUSIC SYNTHESIZERS (1)

Audio Oscillators 74
Control Systems 75
Frequency Modulation 77
Oscillator Mixers 79
Voltage-Controlled Amplifiers 80
Amplitude Modulation 83

CHAPTER 6: ELECTRONIC MUSIC SYNTHESIZERS (2)

Low-Pass Filter 89
High-Pass Filter 91
Band-Pass Filter 92
Band-Reject Filter 93
Fixed Filter Bank 93
Program Equalizers 94
Voltage-Controlled Filters 95
Regeneration 96
Random-Signal Generators 96
Reverberation Units 98

CHAPTER 7: ELECTRONIC MUSIC SYNTHESIZERS (3)

Ring Modulation   101
Sample-and-Hold   103
Analog Sequencers   105
Summary   112

APPENDIX: IN THE STUDIO

From Chapter 3:

    Study # 1: Experiments in Tape Speed and Direction   115
    Study # 2: Creating Composite Sounds   116
    Study # 3: Tape Loops   117
    Study # 4: Sound-on-Sound   118
    Study # 5: Tape Echo   118
    Study # 6: A Composition of Musique Concrète   119

From Chapters 4 and 5:

    Study # 1: Bach Chorale "Now Thank We All
               Our God" (first version)   120
    Study # 2: Bach Chorale (second version)   125
    Study # 3: "Electrophunk in A"   126

Glossary of Terms Frequently Used in Electronic Music   133

Index   139

PREFACE

Never in the history of music has there been a period of such radical change as the twentieth century, and no other single development in that time has had the effect on the music listener and the impact on the state of the art than that of electronic music. Although the use of electrical energy for the creation of music goes back to the turn of the century, the genesis of today's electronic music was probably the work of the *Groupe de Recherche de Musique Concrète* begun in Paris at the close of World War II. It was with the works of these composers, using tape recorders and the studio facilities of Radio-Diffusion Française, that serious electronic music actually had its start.

Within barely a quarter of a century, the fascination with this new musical material has spread throughout the world. Electronic music studios exist in almost every nation, some privately owned, some state subsidized, some operated by industry or by universities. Many hundreds of college facilities are now training students in electronic music production, composition, and education. It would be impossible to turn on an American radio or television without hearing electronic music in commercials, station identifications, or background scoring. Totally embraced by the youth of today, it plays a major role in current popular music, rock, and jazz. At the same time, it has become a vital force in the field of concert music, and has become widely incorporated into theater and dance.

Paralleling the rapid growth of electronic music has been the close association of other art forms with their technological counterparts. Entirely new and unique esthetics have developed relating to such combinations of art and technology as computer graphics, holography, kinetic sculpture, light art, and multimedia.

The developments in the field of electronics over these years have greatly facilitated the manipulation and modification of sound. The availability of voltage-controlled systems (referred to here by their more common name, *synthesizers*) has shortened by many hours the compositional procedures followed by the originators of *musique concrète.* In more recent years, computer technology has been applied to the generation of musical sounds. Technological advancements, however, do not assure esthetic quality. The most sophisticated synthesizers, in uncreative hands, will not, magically, create valid music. Many fine works, however, have come out of simple "cellar" studios with minimal equipment setups.

Electronic music should not be considered a specific style. It is, in fact, a complex musical instrument much the same as a symphony orchestra. Just as we don't consider orchestral music good simply because it is orchestral music, we must resist the flirtation with the unusual which assures us that electronic music is good because it's electronic.

We assume that the reader already has a basic musical background and a familiarity with musical terminology. We begin with Why? and explore the turbulence of twentieth-century music in general, concentrating on those elements that have most strongly influenced electronic music. The historical material, including a short history of electronic musical instruments, is intended only to provide a perspective for creative ideas and creative listening. We shall stress the introduction to terminology, equipment, and concepts unique to the field of electronic music. The explanations—simple, logical, and non-mathematical—are aimed at providing an understanding of the *functions* of tape recorders and electronic music synthesizers as well as the *applications* of these functions to basic musical composition procedures.

Chapters III, V, VI and VII, which deal with tape recording and the synthesizers, are directly correlated to Appendix I. This appendix provides a series of exercises and studies "In the Studio" and is accompanied by a recording that demonstrates possible solutions to each exercise.

1

TODAY'S MUSICAL VOCABULARY

There was a game that we used to play as undergraduate music students, which consisted of playing little-known works of Mozart and Haydn for each other and trying to guess which of the two was the composer. It was a difficult task, not because the composers of the classical period lacked individuality (far from it!), but because their individual tastes played only a small and subtle role in the larger picture of a style determined by and within a limited musical vocabulary.

It would be inaccurate to suggest that their musical vocabulary was undeveloped. In fact, it had already been clearly delineated during the seventeenth century, molded by the masters of Baroque instrumental music, and cast to perfection by J. S. Bach. The limitations were imposed through the decrees of "good taste" which, in late eighteenth-century musical circles, were defined rather rigidly.

Good taste is immensely difficult to explain, since it depends on many external factors—social, economic, political, ethnic, and philosophic. The determinants of style in the mid-eighteenth century were the tastes of a relatively few sophisticated concert and theater patrons in the major cities of Europe. They represented a new upper middle class of professionals, intellectuals, and dilettantes who demanded logic and formal clarity in music, art, and theater. The response of the writers, artists, and composers of that time was the artistic product we now call *classicism*.

One can clearly draw a parallel between the emergence of individual self-awareness following the American and French revolutions and the loosening of the conventions imposed upon the musical vocabulary for the hundred years that followed the age of Mozart and Haydn. As the freedom to employ more "radical" harmonic, melodic, formal, and orchestral devices increased in proportion to the taste for self-expression, individual styles became more and more unique. The romanticism of the nineteenth century produced composers searching for individual outlets for emotion, for a "beauty" that would appeal to the greater numbers of people who now attended concerts, ballets, and operas. Often this search ended in a compromise with sentimentality, a solution with a definite appeal for the mass audience.

One aspect of romanticism was its fascination with things non-Western. Originally a superficial attempt to achieve an exotic character within a work of art, in many cases, the artist or composer had no first-hand knowledge of the culture from which he was borrowing. But thanks to this fascination with the exotic, combined with rapid developments in travel, trade, and industry, by the late nineteenth century the music, arts and artifacts of most of the world had found their way into the museums and collections of Europe.

The French musician Claude Debussy made the most significant breakthrough into "modern" music of any single composer of his day. He had, in essence, exhausted the vocabulary of the past two centuries and, by imposing newly discovered techniques of Oriental melody and timbre on the existing harmonic schemes, he created the first of the new musical vocabularies.

The music of the twentieth century has embraced numerous and radical changes from the vocabulary of traditional Western music. Starting with the *impressionism* of Debussy, we will now examine some of the major influences (often societal and technological) on both popular and concert music. Throughout these discussions, emphasis will be on those factors contributing to the acceptance of electronic music in today's musical vocabulary.

IMPRESSIONISM
THE DISCOVERY OF SOUND AS COLOR

Impressionism was an art movement dealing with such visual images as sun-drenched colors, blurred or hinted outlines of shapes, the dynamic effect of light, shadow, and reflections—all conceived of to create a glimpse of a subject, to stop time as with a camera, but without the cold reality of the photographic image.

Claude Debussy did not think of music, and especially his music, as "impressionistic." However, looking back, we can see many characteristics of his work which parallel the esthetics of the visual artists, and it is generally agreed that if any musician was an impressionist, it was Debussy. His sympathy with the objectives of the impressionists—love of color and light, unclear outlines, subtle shifts of mood—make him the first of the "new vocabulary" composers. "Of all the musicians who ever lived, Claude Debussy was one of the most original and most adventurous—he made music that diverged radically from the common practice of his predecessors."[1]

One of the most striking aspects of the music of Debussy is the type of pitch organizations (scales) that he used. Borrow·ing from the exotic Balinese orchestras (*gamelans*), he freely employed scales of only five or six tones which, when used melodically, would create a flow of line independent of a classical harmonic scheme. He also delved far into the past to incorporate scales from the Middle Ages. These were the "Ecclesiastical Modes," long since replaced by the major-minor system upon which all classical harmony is based.

By employing these unusual pitch organizations, Debussy so altered the harmonies of his music that they no longer moved in the "logical" progressions of the classical or romantic composers. Freed from conformity, he could explore harmonic forms unrelated to those of classical music and permit harmony to function in a new and unique manner.

Before Debussy, a chord was an integral part of a system of movement. Any dissonance was used to create tension and (by the process known as resolution) relaxation within the pattern of chords conceived of as the *harmonic progression.*

3

With Debussy's "impressionism," a dissonant chord could stand by itself as a single entity . . . a mood . . . a *color.* Instrumentation became the method of producing these musical colors in all their possible shades. *He "played" his orchestration in much the same way as today's composer "plays" a synthesizer—by choosing the instrumentation according to overtones, fundamental tones, and the possibilities of color combinations.* ". . . He was special because he was better than any others playing the same game. The game can be called *sound,* sound taking precedence over shape, even language."[2]

As the impressionist painters explored color on their canvases, so Debussy changed chords and melodies to elements of musical color. As the painters obscured the outlines of their subjects by shading one color into another, so Debussy obscured his formal outlines with irregular cadences and melodic elisions. As the painters evoked an image of one specific instance of time, so Debussy, through his suspension of the harmonic progression, seemed to make a greater schism between "musical time" and "real time" than had ever existed in Western music.

The greatest success of all for Debussy's music was its immense popularity and the spread of his musical ideas throughout the world. Those ideas virtually put an end to the production of classical and romantic music by the time of his death in 1918.

SERIALISM AND ATONALITY
ORGANIZATION v. INSPIRATION

Vienna has been the cradle of two major movements in Western music. The first was the emergence of the classical style, exemplified by the Viennese composers Mozart, Haydn, and Beethoven. The waltz era of the Strausses notwithstanding, the second "Viennese school" was that of the early twentieth century, when Arnold Schoenberg and his students Alban Berg and Anton Webern developed the concept of *serialization.*

Serialized music began with Schoenberg as 12-tone organization. He had been composing in the highly chromatic style of

4

the late romantic period, and had realized that his work, with its continual "key" modulations, wide melodic movement, and rich orchestration, appeared to be the final possible extensions of the existing vocabulary. By 1910, he had begun to employ certain arbitrary decisions in his composition process that would alter the amount of "classicism" in his vocabulary:

1. Avoidance of octaves, thirds, or sixths as melodic leaps *or* harmonic intervals
2. Avoidance of more than a few notes in succession from *any one* scale or chord

Obviously what Schoenberg was striving for was an escape from tonality. For another ten years, he explored the areas of nontonal music and developed such techniques as *sprechstimme* (a vocal style of half sung, half spoken phrases gliding from point to point in a highly dramatic manner). In 1922 he unfolded his entire 12-tone style in a suite for piano.

The notes of a serialized composition relate not to a tonal center, but only to each other. In order to achieve this, certain preparations are made before the actual composition is written. Principally, they consist of the creation of a *matrix*. The notes to be used as the thematic basis of the composition (usually the 12 tones of the chromatic scale) are arranged in some desired order. This "row" is called the *original row*. For example, the original row for Schoenberg's Suite for Piano is as follows:

E F G Db Gb Eb Ab D B C A Bb

This row is used with strict controls limiting the repetition of notes and determining that all notes are to be used within each statement of a row. The row is also played from back to front, an order called the *retrograde*. It is also possible to "invert" each interval from the first note. For instance, the interval of E to F (a minor second up) would become E to Eb (a minor second down) in its inversion. The matrix from which serialized tonal material may be taken is created by writing out the original row from left to right, writing the inversion from top to bottom, beginning with the first note of the orginal, and writing out the transpositions of each note of the inversion

5

from left to right. The matrix of Schoenberg's Suite for Piano can be represented as follows:

ORIGINAL →   ← RETROGRADE

	E	F	G	Db	Gb	Eb	Ab	D	B	C	A	Bb	
Eb	E	Gb	C	F	D	G	Db	Bb	B	Ab	A		→ Transposition
Db	D	E	Bb	Eb	C	F	B	Ab	A	Gb	G		→ Transposition
G	Ab	Bb	E	A	Gb	B	F	D	Eb	C	Db		→ Transposition
D	Eb	F	B	E	Db	Gb	C	A	Bb	G	Ab		→ Transposition
F	Gb	Ab	D	G	E	A	Eb	C	Db	Bb	B		→ Transposition
C	Db	Eb	A	D	B	E	Bb	G	Ab	F	Gb		→ Transposition
Gb	G	A	Eb	Ab	F	Bb	E	Db	D	B	C		→ Transposition
A	Bb	C	Gb	B	Db	Db	G	E	F	D	Eb		→ Transposition
Ab	A	B	F	Bb	G	C	Gb	Eb	E	Db	D		→ Transposition
Cb	C	D	Ab	Db	Bb	Eb	A	Gb	G	E	F		→ Transposition
Bb	Cb	Db	G	C	A	D	Ab	F	Gb	Eb	E		→ Transposition

(Left margin, top to bottom: INVERSION ↓; then RETROGRADE INVERSION ↑)

From the material of the matrix, the composer of serial music creates melody and "harmony," depending upon whether the row is used horizontally or vertically. Through the careful preparation of a matrix, the composer is able to determine many intervallic and linear elements of a composition before he begins. More recently, composers have employed computers to determine the best matrix possibilities, and have created similar matrices to determine loudness, rhythmic notation, and even instrumentation.

The twentieth century has been a time in which scientific thinking has had considerable impact upon the arts. In serial music it is manifested in a movement toward "total organiza-

6

tion"; the development of the theories of chance too have their musical counterpart, as we shall discover later in this chapter.

Much early electronic music, and almost all computer music, has been strongly influenced by those composers who, having themselves been involved with techniques of total organization, look upon the instrumentation of electronics as a means of furthering their ability to "control" sound rather than "play" it.

DADAISM
THE BREAKDOWN OF THE "LOGICAL" IN ART

In the spring of 1916, Europe was in the throes of World War I. Man's intellect and creativity had gone into the development of technology and science, and now the battlefields were covered with the dead, victims of poison gas, aerial bombing, machine guns, long range artillery, tanks. The tools of the great industrial revolution had been turned to destruction.

In the same spring, the city of Zurich, nestled in neutral Switzerland, was an oasis for many. The money used to finance the war was stored in its banks, as were the profits of war, gathering interest, no doubt, in proportion to the ferocity of the fighting.

Many people had sought refuge in Zurich—the pacifists, artists, writers, and political opponents of the raging war. They gathered in the cafés and coffeehouses to talk, argue, and question the purpose of war, the systems of society, philosophies, and art. In the Cabaret Voltaire, a revolution in creative thinking took shape which, as small as it began and remained, shook the esthetic foundations of painting, sculpture, poetry, and music.

In this café, five or six artists regularly presented a review consisting of music, skits, and poetry. The material was often antiwar, but more often antiestablishment, the absurdity of the shows themselves reflecting the artists' view of the absurdity of the state of the world. A French singer named Madame LeRoy was booked to perform at the Cabaret Voltaire. In the search for a stage name, the word *dada* (a child's word for rocking horse) was chosen at random from a French dictionary. We

7

know not whether Madame LeRoy herself was a success, but *dada* soon came to be associated with the artistic philosophy of the Cabaret Voltaire, and within a few years dadaism was a recognized movement in the world of art. Dadaist manifestos appeared throughout Europe and the United States.

Dadaism is often referred to as an "antiart" movement because of its emphasis on the absurd. A typical dadaist "concert" consisted of the simultaneous reading of poetry in four or five languages, or the reading of a poem consisting only of the letter *W*. (Copies were, of course, given to the audience so that they could "follow" the text.) One dada sculpture, the complete negation of classic function, was a flatiron with sharp steel spikes affixed to its face, which would, of course, destroy anything ironed by it.

In reality, the freedom from previous restrictions imposed upon the arts lent itself to contemporary expressions in sculpture, to the concept of "collage" (the application of more than one texture to a surface), and to the employment of mass (or "pop") culture in a work of fine art. Possibly of greatest importance was the breakdown of the classical concept of logic which, still residual from the eighteenth century, had continued to dominate artistic thinking.

The dadaist period was the first in modern history in which artists clearly equated the state of mankind's achievements with the state of its arts and concluded that by destroying the barriers imposed by the tastes of a "distasteful" society, they could pave the way for new forms of expression.

Dadaism fostered two important musical developments. One—a marked rebellion against the popular bombastic quality of Western music, as exemplified by the followers of Wagner—was an outgrowth of the works of Eric Satie, the only dada composer, with his use of simplistic devices and folk and "pop" material.

The second—directly related to the eventual development of electronic music—was the use of noise (*bruitism,* as developed by the Italian and French dadaists) as part of a musical performance. The noises of the society, ranging from human shouting to airplane engines, were included in compositions as structural entities. (One famous example was George Antheil's *Ballet*

Mécanique staged in 1926 in Paris and New York.) In sculpture, objects were exhibited as "found art" (art trouvé). This concept was to become, with the invention of tape recording, the important development called *musique concrète,* which we will discuss in detail later in this book.

SILENCE AND SONORITY
A REDEFINITION OF MUSICAL TIME

Closely linked to the widespread interest in serial organization which developed during the 1920s, and not without influence from the dadaists, a new sense of musical time began to develop which now plays a vital role in all areas of contemporary music, from the concert hall to the television commercial. It is easy to see how this relates to the breakdown of the classical traditions, and how, of all the techniques of today's music, it is the most difficult for most people to grasp.

Of all the elements in the musical vocabulary, time is the most basic. Music *must* exist in time. Printed music can only be a representation of the *passage of time combined with the perception of sound* which we call the musical experience. Most Western music employs organizations of time within the framework of repeated regular *beats.* This division of time into beat patterns is common to most of the world's music. The music of the West has further limited these beat patterns by placing them within the framework of regular accented *metric* structures called *measures.* By the end of the nineteenth century, the metric patterns of Western music had become almost entirely limited to simple meters divisible by two or three ($\frac{2}{4}, \frac{3}{4}, \frac{4}{4}, \frac{2}{2}, \frac{6}{8}, \frac{9}{8}$, etc.).

As the twentieth century developed, certain influences began to play upon rhythmic organization. For one thing, the non-Western music which had affected the tonal writing of Debussy had also influenced the *rhythmic* composition of Stravinsky. Early Stravinsky ballets, such as *The Rite of Spring,* include sections in which meter is changed in every measure! Such irregularity creates excitement *by removing the predict-*

ability of classical meter and leaving the listener unsure of the beat patterns of the work. (This was also an approximation of what Stravinsky considered "primitive" rhythms.)

Anton Webern was a pupil of Schoenberg's. As well as adopting the system of tonal serialization, he also experimented with the serialization of rhythmic elements. By placing arbitrary controls over the rhythms of a piece, he created totally new concepts of meter. Webern used precise and subtle structures, often very short and soft. In order to make each sound important enough to stand on its own, he employed long periods of silence between them. His textures are transparent, and when one listens to his music, it is not the *melody* that one relates to, but the juxtapositions of silences and sonorities.

The sonorities of Webern's music are often extremely delicate; a single note can stand isolated in a world of silence. The listener's attention is shifted from one event to another while each sound becomes the satisfaction of the previous sound. Time, in Webern's music, is not easily perceived by the listener as beats. Instead, the use of sound-events as focal points leaves one with a feeling of *spatial time*. This may be defined as a kind of free-floating, nonmetric passage of time unrelated to harmony and meter, depending only upon the relationship of "events" to one another.

Possibly the most startlingly radical, avant-garde, and isolated composer of the twentieth century was Edgard Varèse. Born in Paris in 1885, he first pursued an interest in mathematics and engineering, deciding to study music seriously only after he had turned nineteen. Although he studied at the very traditional Paris Conservatory, traditionalism was never to be a part of his vocabulary. He moved to New York's Greenwich Village in 1915 and lived there until his death in 1965, when he was hailed as the greatest single influence on the musical avant-garde. Today, his disciples range from university composers to rock-oriented musicians such as Frank Zappa.

Varèse was concerned primarily with the combination of rhythmic and timbral elements in his music. His "harmonies" were generally extremely dissonant, and he seldom followed the chord progressions of traditional music. He was not willing to comply with any single compositional dictate, and therefore

10

never followed the road to serialism. His organization was built upon the structures of sounds—"events"—and he called his music *organized sound*.

Although Varèse could not in any sense be considered a prolific composer, each of his works displays the total dedication to concept from which he never swayed. Between 1920 and 1937, he composed only 11 works. *Ionisation* (1931) was the first modern composition for percussion alone, and employed sirens in an attempt to produce pitched sound which was variable in frequency and nonmelodic—an escape from the dominance of traditional instrumental color. *Density 21.5* (1936) was composed for unaccompanied flute. The performer for whom he wrote the piece played a platinum flute, and the title refers to the specific gravity of platinum.

Other titles of Varèse's music (*Hyperprism, Integrales, Metal*) show an obvious interest in the physical properties of things and the general "scientism" with which he was fascinated. Just before World War II, he traveled to Paris to inquire about the possibility of using some sort of recording device as an instrument for composition. What he wanted to do was to manipulate and modify sounds electronically. Tape recorders had been developed, but were not generally accepted or available. Within five years after the end of the war, the tape recorder became available to the public, and Varèse's first tape piece, *Deserts,* was begun in 1951.

A new flurry of compositional activity sprang forth from the ever exploring mind of Edgard Varèse, sparking the era of his only popular success, the music for the Philips pavilion at the Brussels World's Fair of 1957. After considerable argument with the Philips company over the suitability of the work, the designer of the pavilion, the world-renowned Le Corbusier, insisted that the Varèse work, 480 seconds long for 400 loudspeakers, be performed if he (Le Corbusier) were to design the building.

The last ten years of Varèse's life was a period in which his presence at concerts of contemporary music caused whispers of excitement in the audience. After one program, at the New York Avant-Garde Festival, Varèse and his wife were having coffee at the Carnegie Tavern with festival promoter Norman

Seaman. Seaman suggested that they look in the early editions of the morning newspapers for reviews. Not only were the reviews enthusiastic, but most of them contained glowing tributes to Varèse's influence on the younger generation of composers. After listening silently to the columns of praise, Varèse smiled, then began to laugh aloud, and leaning to his wife, said in French, "After all those years of their throwing dung on me, I suppose that I've finally become a fertilizer."

ALEATORY AND IMPROVISATION
THEORIES OF CHANCE AND INDETERMINACY

In apparent opposition to concepts of "total organization," a small but highly publicized group of composers have, since the late thirties and early forties, championed the idea of "indeterminate" music. There are two basic types of indeterminate music ... *improvisation* is indeterminate only to the listener, since the player or players are quite in control of the environment. The other, *aleatory,* is more sophisticated, and the methods used to assure indeterminancy are either mathematical (random-number computer programs) or philosophic (the *I Ching,* or Chinese Book of Changes).

The forces of determining the musical arts have always moved as a pendulum between precise logical organization and sensuous expression. In the classical era of Mozart and Haydn, as you probably know, the pendulum leaned toward the organized side. As the romantic age developed, the pendulum swung toward the sensuous again. Needless to say, every *great* composer has employed a bit of both areas, seasoning his composition, as it were, with a sprinkling of the less popular. Mozart's introspection and lyricism as well as Wagner's careful use of counterpoint are good examples.

In the twentieth century, the tremendous growth in communication technologies, the effects of mass educational concepts, the great leveling of social class structures, and the ever-growing numbers of "artists" and audiences have had a staggering effect upon this pendulum. The oscillations of the style pendulum has been changing so rapidly that, like the markings of a stroboscope the pendulum seems either to stand still or to be in all places at once. A concert today might include aleatoric music by John Cage, a serialized work by Stefan Wolpe, an electronic piece by Bulent Arel, and an improvisation by Lukas Foss.

Aleatory is a term widely used in musical circles. Originally derived from the Latin word for gambling, it is often used to denote something achieved by the throw of dice. Aleatoric music includes elements of chance in both composition and performance. Many composers have incorporated aleatoric areas in their music, but none has done this with the philosophical determination of the American contemporary, John Cage.

There is a good bit of the dadaist in Cage, but it would be quite inaccurate to pass off his work as "absurd." In his earlier nonchance period, he is noted for the *Preludes and Interludes for Prepared Piano*. In these works, the piano had to be "prepared" before performance. This preparation included the use of nuts and bolts attached to strings, rubber erasers and various bits of hardware on the hammers, and so forth. The effect of this "preparation" was a sound unique to each piece and not unlike the sounds of Oriental instruments. After establishing himself in the musical avant-garde with these pieces, Cage ventured into the area of indeterminacy with such pieces as *Imaginary Landscapes* (for 24 radios) and 4'33" (a piano piece in which the performer sits at the piano for four minutes and thirty three seconds without playing).

In 1966, a work was produced for the Merce Cunningham Dancers and performed at Philharmonic Hall in New York. It represented the wedding of aleatory with technology which has become the hallmark of Cage's artistic output. On the stage the dancers moved among a dozen electronic sensing devices. Each of these devices (designed for the performance by R. A. Moog) was to amplify a sound in direct proportion to the distance of a dancer from the five-foot antenna on each device.

Numerous sound sources (radios, tape recorders, oscillators and contact microphones attached to Slinky toys) were fed to these sensors, and the outputs went into a number of mixers at the rear of the stage. At each mixer, a performer chose the

13

desired sounds and then passed his "output" to Cage himself, who was controlling still another "final" mixer. At this point, Cage would, by some choice, determine what sound the audience would hear.

The result of this piece was that the music and the dance were either related or nonrelated. Sounds were either heard or not heard. Cage had demonstrated his own concept of musical rhythm, that of "things and nonthings." He had sought and partially achieved his philosophical goal, the complete submission of the ego and the intellect to the elements of chance.

In a "Profile" in *The New Yorker,* Cage once said that the two musical areas that he liked least were Beethoven and jazz. Since Beethoven represents the expression of the individual ego through classical organization and jazz represents the individual ego through improvisation, this would appear consistent with his thinking.

Improvisation in music has, of course, always existed. Beethoven was said to be a talented improviser himself and Bach was a master! In the nineteenth century, when emotionalism and theatricality were at a peak, many concert artists concluded their programs with elaborate improvisations, either on their own themes or on the popular themes of others. Church organists to this day practice the art of improvisation when they must "fill" certain sections of their services.

Western music, however, has never included improvisation to the extent that Indian music does (where improvisation has become the "classical" means of thematic development)—or African (where improvised situations demand improvised communal responses and where the art of song-story is highly developed). Contemporary experiences with improvisation in Western music have been primarily through jazz.

Improvisation in early jazz consisted first of emotional and expressive interpretations of melody lines directly related to the West African traditions. Instrumental jazz of the early period (1900-20) employed group improvisations based on familiar tunes, with little use of solos. In the 1920s, the solo styles appeared, and improvising became the skill of creating new melodies over known chord patterns. As modern jazz began to develop, chord patterns became more sophisticated and were

14

often borrowed from Debussy. This change in harmonic concept began to shape more elaborate melodic styles.

In the 1950s, a new concept of improvisation began to emerge in jazz. It was related to a rebirth of Black political activity and was an attempt to combine "African" music with the influence of such contemporaries as Varèse and Cage. This type of improvisation consists of total improvising— referred to in jazz as "the new thing" or "free form." In it, the sensitivity of each musician in the group to his fellow performers must be highly developed. Far from "doing anything you want," free-form improvisation requires considerable preparation, both stylistically and psychologically.

Free-form improvisation outside of jazz has also appeared within the past two decades. It has assumed an extremely important role, especially with works combining improvisation and determinate composition, either for traditional instruments or for electronic tapes. One of the early examples of this style is *Time Cycles* by Lukas Foss. Even the field of educational music has been affected by improvisation, and a number of high school and even elementary school band and choral works include elements of free or limited improvisation.

CONCLUSION – ECLECTICISM
THE WHOLE IS GREATER THAN ITS PARTS

If, 200 years from now, music students are playing the same guessing game that we played, applying their skills to the twentieth century, it's unlikely that they'll have great difficulty telling Milton Babbitt, say, from John Cage. Both are often involved with electronic music, but each chooses his material from an entirely different vocabulary. Cage employs the electronic devices of contact microphones, random noise amplification, and "tape mixes" of unrelated materials. His vocabulary is aleatory. Babbitt, on the other hand, chooses highly complex rhythmic structures, serialized melodies, and a composition style of tightly organized precision. His choice of electronic composition instruments is the RCA synthesizer, which is "programmed" in short musical events by means of punched tape.

15

In the 1960s, some composers became attracted by the "live-plus-electronic" area of composition. Performances of purely taped music lack visual elements—leaving audiences deprived of a total experience. Besides the theatrical implications of combining live and recorded music, there is also a significant esthetic quality to be achieved by juxtaposing both elements in performance. The "man v. machine" conflict takes on interesting proportions, and this interplay has been very successfully handled by such composers as Luciano Berio, Mario Davidowsky, and John Cage.

Combining elements of live and recorded performance has often led to the use of multiple styles, and even vocabularies, in a single piece. A composer might employ serialism in one section of a work to achieve the effect of total organization, and juxtapose this with an area of improvisation, spatially oriented electronic sounds, and so on. The result is an *eclectic* piece which borrows from many areas.

Although frequently criticized as invalid or lacking roots, eclectic music has been widely accepted in both the concert and rock music areas. Eclecticism is an important element in The Beatles' *Sgt. Pepper* album, in much of the work of the Mothers of Invention, occasionally in the music of Blood, Sweat and Tears, Chicago, or Keith Emerson, and in the contemporary jazz of Miles Davis and Chick Corea.

The young composer should note, however, that eclecticism may be the most difficult of all new vocabularies. Its success depends upon a combination of dramatic and rhythmic senses which may have to be developed more critically than in the past. To bring order out of seemingly unrelated materials or vocabularies demands that the effects and techniques of each of the parts be thoroughly understood and that the concept of the whole be clearly predetermined.

Neither the concert music nor the popular music of today has developed in a vacuum. "The past is in the present." In our age, however, the past often refers not to the last century, but to last year, last month ... even last week! Today's composer must accept that what's *new* is not automatically *good*. Yet in a world of highly developed technology this is sometimes difficult.

The young composer of electronic music should become familiar with today's musical vocabulary. It's not enough to sit before a synthesizer and plunge into an aural "freakout." Every aspect of today's music has its roots. In this chapter, I have omitted a great deal and generalized considerably in order to present a handful of the roots present in most electronic music.

The electronic music synthesizer offers more choice of color, shading, and timbral nuance than any instrument of the past. It is more easily adapted to precise programming and control than any of its predecessors. It is capable of producing sounds of great beauty as well as great absurdity! It lends itself to improvisation far beyond the imaginations of Franz Liszt or Jelly Roll Morton.

To consider electronic music of value, simply because it is electronic and therefore something "current" (that pun is hard to resist) is no less facetious than to argue *against* the validity of electronic music simply because it is "made by a machine rather than by a person."

Electronic music has logically evolved out of the musical directions of the past 75 years. One should not lose sight of these directions in an attempt to erase the stigma of "classicism" in a weak attempt at novelty. Every composer in every style mentioned in this chapter has dealt with the problems of relating creative output to contemporary society. *Their* solutions have become part of *our* modern artistic heritage.

NOTES

1. William W. Austin, *Music in the Twentieth Century* (New York: W. W. Norton, 1966) p. 1.

2. Ned Rorem, "Notes on Debussy," in *Pure Contraption* (New York: Holt, Rinehart & Winston, 1974).

2

A SHORT HISTORY OF ELECTRONIC MUSIC

DEVELOPMENTS BEFORE WORLD WAR II

Experimentation with electronic musical instruments parallels the development of the electronics field in the twentieth century. Not until after World War II, however, was electronic music to come into its own. Three factors were probably most important to the emergence of this valid new art form: (1) the end of a major war, with the period of artistic and intellectual efforts which followed, (2) the widespread acceptance of the changes in the musical vocabulary as it had developed early in the century and (3) the availability of radio broadcasting equipment, especially magnetic tape recorders.

Musical machines are not new. They can be traced back to the ancient Greeks, whose *hydraulis,* a water-pressure-operated reed organ, was invented some 300 years before the birth of Christ. Mechanical musical clocks adorned the towers of Europe in the late Middle Ages and were popular during the period of classical Western music. Beethoven himself composed a work (the *Battle* Symphony) for a mechanical instrument, a complex combination of percussion, reeds, and brasses designed by Maelzel, the inventor of the metronome. Only a few photographs of some of the parts of this *panharmonican* now exist. The instrument was destroyed in the bombings of WW II. The *Battle* Symphony, however, is usually considered one of Beethoven's weakest compositions.

It should not be surprising, therefore, that the combination of the acoustical research of Helmholtz during the late nineteenth century and the rapid developments in electricity and related mechanics at that time produced some interest in the design of an electrical musical instrument. What must be considered the first "synthesizer" was build between 1896 and 1906 by American inventor Thaddeus Cahill.

Cahill's musical machine was called the Telharmonium. Its similarity to the modern synthesizer lies in its basic concept, certainly not in its size or even its mode of operation. In fact, the tremendous size of the Telharmonium may be hard to imagine. When it was completed and moved to New York for installation, it weighed over two hundred tons and took up several railroad flatcars. The reason for its mammoth size was the complex machinery used to generate current at sufficient levels to operate the mechanical speaker cones.

The "oscillators" were a series of rapidly spinning "alternators," driven by electric motors and producing alternating currents at fixed frequencies. (Those frequencies were dependent upon the speed of the drive motors and a series of pulleys, belts, and gears which varied the speeds in proportion to the chromatic tunings of a piano keyboard.) There were separate alternators for the fundamental tones and the first six overtones, and although filtering as we know it (and shall discuss it in later chapters) was not used on the Telharmonium, the *spectrum* of a particular tone could be shaped using separate overtone controls. The instrument was polyphonic, at least to two or three voices, and had a touch-sensitive keyboard.

Apart from being immensely cumbersome and expensive, the Telharmonium required two "performers" and was so noisy it had to be housed in a room separate from the speakers. The acoustical quality of the speaker system designed for it was, by high-fidelity standards, quite poor, and provoked comments about the "exaggerated, growling effects of chords closely grouped in the bass."[1]

The New York Electric Music Company was established to sell music produced by the Telharmonium on a subscription basis by telegraph wires. Stockholders of this enterprise foresaw thousands of people acquiring receivers and dialing concerts of

20

electrical music into their parlors—a commercial concept not unlike that of today's cable TV promotions. Despite the praises of many prophetic people in the arts, however, the Telharmonium and the New York Electric Music Company failed and have been all but forgotten.

Just at the time that Cahill's Telharmonium was completed, and the N.Y.E.M.C. was setting up its business ventures, inventions in the design of vacuum tubes were rendering many of Cahill's principles obsolete. In 1904, Fleming patented the "radio valve" or diode tube, and in 1915, the triode tube was patented by De Forrest. This device made possible the construction of electrical amplifiers, and began the age of electronics.

By far the most successful of the early electronic instruments was the Theremin. Invented between 1920 and 1924 by Russian designer Leon Theremin, and originally called the Etherophone or Thereminovox, it is known today by the name of its inventor.

The success of the Theremin was due largely to its method of performance. It is the only musical instrument that is played without being touched. The performer, standing in front of the Theremin and moving his or her hands in the air before two antennae rising from the instrument, can control both the pitch and the volume. Theremins are designed so that the right-hand antenna controls pitch and the left-hand antenna controls volume.

The Theremin employs two oscillators of very high inaudible frequencies. One of these is fixed, and the other changes its frequency in response to the minute changes in capacitance of the player's body when placed close to the antenna. The *sound* that is produced is a *third* frequency that occurs when the first two interact. I would suggest that after gaining familiarity with this text, and with synthesizers in general, you read the opening material in Chapter VII dealing with ring modulation and compare that to the operation of the Theremin. See also, "A Transistorized Theremin," by R. A. Moog, in *Electronics World,* January 1961.

The Theremin became quite popular in the late twenties. It was patented in the United States in 1928, and during the thirties was built and promoted in the United States by RCA

21

(without much success). Theremins are being built today, and for ten years prior to the invention of his own synthesizer, Robert A. Moog was one of the leading designers of these instruments.

There are two major problems with the Theremin as a musical instrument: (1) it is almost impossible to articulate accurately, that is, produce clean attacks and smooth, even decays and (2) it is virtually impossible for those without an excellent relative (or "absolute") sense of pitch to play in tune. A hand in the air produces no fixed reference point between notes, intervals, or octaves. All must be done "by ear."

Leon Theremin was commissioned by a number of prominent composers during the thirties to produce other electronic instruments. He made an improved Theremin for Edgard Varèse in 1934, and an instrument called a Rhythmicon in 1931, for the composer Henry Cowell. The Rhythmicon was the prototype for the many electronic rhythm instruments that began to appear commercially *thirty years later*. Like the most recent ones, it could produce any standard rhythm as well as combine rhythms in complex patterns.

Probably the most successful of all electronic musical instruments was the organ invented in 1935 by Laurens Hammond. In many ways, this instrument was similar to the Cahill Telharmonium, using an electromechanical tone generator of almost the same concept as Cahill's of forty years earlier. Hammond modernized the system by greatly reducing its size, and by employing the electronic amplifiers and more sensitive speaker systems by that time available. He employed many units of his own design, including a synchronous drive motor originally built for other nonmusical applications (T. L. Rhea's *Evolution of Electronic Musical Instruments* discusses this interesting invention in more detail). One of the most important features of the Hammond organ were the draw-bars with which the performer could add or subtract overtones from the fundamental being played on the keyboard. These were designed to produce not only traditional organlike sonorities, but also tones with harmonics occurring in proportions not found in any acoustical instrument.

Widespread development of the popular music industry

22

during the late thirties helped to make the Hammond organ the hottest musical instrument of the swing era. It became so popular that for many years the name Hammond was almost synonymous with electronic organ. Organ records were highly promoted and artists became specialists in the performance of jazz and popular music on the Hammond. In the commercial sense, the age of electronic music was already upon us.

The Hammond corporation was also responsible for two other electronic instruments popular in the jazz, pop, and recording fields during the early forties. These were the Solovox and the Novachord. The Solovox was a monophonic instrument capable of playing only one note at a time, with a keyboard about two and a half octaves in length. It was often attached below the keyboard of a piano, just to the right of the player, enabling him to switch it on and perform an electronic solo line while accompanying himself with his left hand on the piano keyboard. The Novachord was a more interesting instrument. It was polyphonic, and incorporated preset timbres designed to reproduce many of the traditional acoustical instruments. It was first received with considerable interest, but intonation and performance problems limited its sales, and it was discontinued after a few years of production.

Probably the most important of the European electronic keyboard instruments during the thirties was the Ondes Martenot, designed in 1929 by Maurice Martenot. This instrument, regularly employed by the more serious composer, like Varèse, Messiaen, or Honegger, became popular in the American recording studios during the early 1950s. For use on radio and television commercials, the Martenot predated synthesizers by a good ten years.

In 1939, John Cage composed the first of a series of compositions called *Imaginary Landscapes*. In all of these works, he explored the combination of traditionally notated music with elements of chance, or aleatory. These techniques, as described in chapter I, have had a tremendous effect upon the esthetic directions taken by music since then. In Imaginary Landscapes #1, Cage combined live instruments (prepared piano and cymbal) with tones from test oscillators which had been recorded on an RCA test record. In order to perform the piece,

23

two variable-speed record players were needed. Since these were found only in recording studios, the piece was actually intended only for recorded performance. With this work and others like it, Cage established the recorded performance as the final version of a composition, a direction that would be followed by musicians of all musical styles with the advent of tape recording a generation later.

THE TAPE RECORDER AND
MUSIQUE CONCRÈTE

Two Parisians, acoustical engineer Pierre Schaeffer and composer Pierre Henry, were solely responsible for the now well known school of contemporary music called by Schaeffer *musique concrète*. That *musique concrète* was a French development is not surprising. Historically, the French have always been extremely concerned with color and texture in their music. From the eighteenth century, and continuing in an ever-increasing manner into the twentieth, this fascination with timbre, texture, and nuance marks a distinctively nationalistic character of French music. It contrasts noticeably with the Germanic interest in harmonic progression and formal structure and with the Italian emphasis on emotionalism and melodic lyricism. It should be considered in keeping with this tradition for Varèse to have developed his concept of organized sound. In the visual arts, it was the Frenchman Marcel Duchamp who created the idea of *art trouvé*—"found" art. The relationship, while possibly not intentional, would be difficult to overlook. Just as Duchamp "found" objects and displayed them in gallaries or combined them in large "constructions," Schaeffer and Henry "found" their raw material on phonograph records and, superimposing these in their studio, employed *filtering, speed changes* and other recording studio techniques in order to create new "sound constructions."

The primary aim of *musique concrète* is the alteration of the listener's perception. A distinctive sound, such as the noise of an automobile engine, becomes a unique entity when recorded—heard, that is, without the visual aspect of the auto itself. This perceptual change is heightened by the addition of filtering to alter the overtone structure of the original sound. If the recording is played backwards, another marked change takes place, with the sound occurring in a way that it cannot in nature. *Gateing,* or the abrupt starting and stopping of a recorded event, is another device employed in *musique concrète.*

Although the first works of Schaeffer and Henry (1947-48) were produced without the use of a tape recorder, this instrument soon became the most important tool for them and their immediate followers. By 1954, composers such as Stockhausen, Boulez, Milhaud, and Varèse had composed in the Paris studios of Schaeffer and Henry. The studios themselves were subsidized by the French government and maintained by Radiodiffusion-Television Française, the nationalized telecommunications company of France (ORTF).

The compositions produced in these early years of *musique concrète* were, for the most part, not major musical events. The techniques of tape manipulation, splicing, filtering, and electronic alteration of sounds which these composers developed, however, were important to the later work in electronic music. Most important of all was the esthetic concept of recorded musical compositions that finally had begun to give credence to the *bruitists* of dadaism who, in 1920, were imagining a music made of noises instead of instrumental tones.

As a purely creative technique, *musique concrète* is often employed in music education today. It has been found to open the door, through creative experimentation, to the teaching of musical textures, forms, and structures and has proved particularly successful in the junior high and middle schools. It is strongly advised that some *musique concrète* composition precede any synthesizer work, since it performs the double function of teaching the operation of the tape recorder as a musical instrument and introducing the esthetic concepts associated with the organization of sound events into communicable musical structures.

Today's serious composer of electronic music will often incorporate some techniques of *musique concrète*. Prerecorded voices or instruments are often used as a source of sound to be

25

manipulated by the composer and used, along with electronically produced signals, as the principal musical materials of a composition. It has been all but forgotten that in 1951, when the Germans opened their studios in Cologne under the artistic guidance of Eimert and Stockhausen, *musique concrète* was considered a separate musical vocabulary and not to be confused with the new German developments of oscillator-generated sounds. Early writings on these subjects made clear distinctions between *musique concrète* and electronic music.

Since the establishment of these early electronic music studios, the technical developments in the field have gone through three distinct phases. In the first, standard testing and broadcasting equipment was used to generate and modify sound. In the second phase, integrated "synthesizers" were employed instead of the more cumbersome and expensive modular studios. In the third phase of electronic music, digital computers were used as a source of control and sound synthesis. Although this book will concentrate almost entirely on the more popular second phase, a brief discussion of all three will follow.

MODERN ELECTRONIC MUSIC, PHASE I

Philosophically, the Cologne Electronic Music Studio, established in 1951, grew almost directly out of the concepts of total organization started by Schoenberg in the early twenties and continued so strongly by his pupil, Anton Webern. Herbert Eimert, the first director, built an electronic music studio capable of precise controls over all of the parameters of music. To quote Herbert Russcol, from his book *The Liberation of Sound,* "They tackled the problem with Teutonic thoroughness, taking an almost reverent and metaphysical approach to the mathematics and physics involved."[2]

In 1953, the Cologne studio was taken over by Karlheinz Stockhausen, one of the most important figures in post-war music. His electronic music, dating through the fifties and into the early sixties, is marked by the combination of carefully structured electronic events with elements of *musique concrète* and of John Cage-influenced aleatory.

26

In New York, in 1951, Columbia University purchased an Ampex tape recorder for the recording of musical programs. Shortly thereafter, Professors Vladimir Ussachevsky and Otto Leuning of the Columbia Department of Music began to explore its possibilities as an instrument for the composition of electronic music. By October of 1952, enough music had been created electronically at Columbia to warrant a public performance. This concert, held at New York's Museum of Modern Art, caused *Time* magazine to comment, "The twentieth-century instrument is the record machine—the tape recorder."

From that time until the development of small synthesizers in 1964, the Columbia-Princeton Electronic Music Studio, jointly directed by Ussachevsky and Milton Babbitt of Princeton University, became the most important in the United States.

Other studios were built during the fifties in various parts of the world. In Toronto, Hugh LeCain, long an experimenter in electronic sound, was granted development monies from the Canadian government and, together with Myron Schaeffer, built an outstanding studio at the University of Toronto. Most electronic music studios in the fifties were either subsidized by government agencies (such as the ORTF Studio in Paris or the Cologne Studio in West Germany) or were built and financed by universities. By this time, however, other uses were being considered for electronic music.

An interesting innovator in an area considered nonserious electronic music was Raymond Scott. Director of an experimental jazz quintet in the late thirties, and later conductor of a highly successful radio and television program, the Lucky Strike Hit Parade, Scott became involved, in the early fifties, with radio commercials (musical jingles). He was one of the first composers in this medium to use a large number of electronic sounds, and his studio, originally housed in his home but later moved to an industrial park on Long Island, contained the most sophisticated recording equipment then available, along with an impressive array of devices for the production of electronic music and *musique concrète*.

As with all "phase I" studios, Scott's consisted of banks of audio oscillators, filters, and gateing devices. It was also equipped with a Hammond organ and an Ondes Martenot, both

27

"built in" to the patching network. Most interesting about the Scott studio, however, were the innovations conceived to speed up the composition process. Raymond Scott seemed to me to be almost compulsively interested in taking some of the work out of composing music. He was, in fact, continuously experimenting with automatic composition devices. After leaving commercial writing, he developed an instrument called the Electronium which, using a complex random selector, produces ever-changing patterns of musical "composition." The most interesting feature of his setup was the completely built-in rhythmical sequencer/gate. Designed sometime during the mid-fifties, it was operated by a series of electromechanical relays, and, though cumbersome by modern standards, worked very well and was far ahead of its time.

With the possible exception of Scott's sequencer and some elaborate tape-loop equipment designed by Hugh LeCain, a tape playing system which varied speed in proportion to "notes" selected on a keyboard—forerunner of the Melotron, most of the composition done in the electronic studios of the 1950s was manually controlled, with many individual recordings made and with tape-splicing the principle organizing factor. In 1959, the RCA Electronic Music Synthesizer Mark II was installed at the Columbia-Princeton studio in New York. With this installation, modern electronic music entered its second phase of development.

MODERN ELECTRONIC MUSIC, PHASE II

Unlike the earlier practice of assembling audio and broadcasting equipment in studios for the purpose of music making, the RCA Mark II was a single instrument designed solely for this purpose. Incorporating a modular concept that allows for far more complex sound structures than had previously been available, the RCA Mark II also has the distinct advantage of being programmable. A binary-coded device on this instrument "reads" the input from a roll of paper which is punched by the composer. The obvious advantage of this is that complete musical events can be set up before performance. The actual performance is, if desired, directly recorded.

28

The establishment of the Columbia-Princeton Electronic Music Studio as America's leading studio during the 1960s was due primarily to the permanent installation of the RCA synthesizer, and partially to a famous public concert of 1961 which stirred up debate on the esthetic validity of electronic music. This debate was widely publicized in the *New York Times* and resulted in considerable interest in the new music in general and the Columbia-Princeton studio in particular.

Since that time, the Columbia-Princeton studio has attracted composers and students from throughout the world, and although many universities in the New York area now house electronic music facilities, the majority of concert works and film scores produced by New York composers have been made (or "realized," as they prefer to say) at this studio.

1963–1965, A PERSONAL RECOLLECTION

In the spring of 1962, I completed a piece for chorus, brass quartet, and tape-recorded *musique concrète*. This work, "Good Friday," was first performed by the Hofstra University Chorus, for whom it was composed, at the Cathedral of the Incarnation, the diocesan center of the Long Island Episcopal Church. The effect of the piece on the audience (it was the first electronic music most of them had heard) was a good one, and I became hooked on the medium.

During the following year, I accumulated various equipment in my family's TV and recreation room. By the fall of 1963, Jason Seley, a sculptor and teaching colleague, had planned a concert to feature my newest pieces. (Jason Seley's work established the style of modern sculpture using welded automobile bumpers as the medium. His work has achieved much recognition and he has since become the Chairman of Fine Arts at Cornell.) Included on the program was a piece called "Contours and Improvisations for Sculpture and Tape Recorder." This was a solo piece for a percussionist, playing on Seley's sculpture to the accompaniment of a tape of *musique concrète* and electronic sounds. Two other new electronic pieces were also composed for that concert.

29

Coincidentally, I had become an instructor at Hofstra University in the fall of 1963, and had been asked to attend a statewide conference of music teachers being held in November at the Eastman School in Rochester. At that conference, while looking at the exhibit booths, I met Robert Moog. He had set up a very modest display in an attempt to publicize a do-it-yourself kit version of the Theremin.

I told Moog that I had bought one of his kits, had "done-it-myself," and had used the instrument as part of the sound sources for my upcoming concert at Jason Seley's Greenwich Village studio. We talked for an hour about my work, his work, the state of electronic music, and the need for new instrumentation. The concert was held in January of 1964, and Moog came to New York to attend and record the program. After the concert, he and I discussed the feasibility of a small, solid-state instrument which could somehow give to a composer some of the possibilities of the Columbia-Princeton studio while being small enough to have in a home and inexpensive enough to afford.

Later that spring, I got a letter from Bob inviting me to spend a few weeks at his shop in Trumansburg, New York. The purpose of the visit was to be the development of his new instrument. I was to act as resident composer. We worked together for two weeks during July of 1964. I spent about eight hours a day improvising, composing, and reacting to Moog's experimentation and technical developments. There was some difficulty, since my knowledge of electronics was minuscule at best, and I invariably expressed my needs in musical terminology which Bob had to reinterpret for himself. We worked with circuits laid out on a table so that they could be constantly changed, modified, and rebuilt. Our first "envelope gateing device" was activated by a 35-cent doorbell button from the local hardware store.

At the end of the two weeks, I had composed a demonstration piece, "Jazz Images" (which is still frequently played), and we performed it for an enthusiastic audience consisting of a handful of local people who worked for Bob on his Theremin kits!

Later that summer Bob put our concepts into concrete form

30

and made a complete prototype instrument. He shipped it to me at my home, and on it I produced some demonstration material for him to use in presenting a paper at the Audio Engineering Society convention that fall.[3] A second prototype was made for the Toronto Electronic Music Studio. During the winter, Moog set up his operation as a twofold affair. He accepted a contract to build inexpensive guitar amplifiers in order to finance the development of the modular electronic music systems.

In the summer of 1965, Robert Moog and I again collaborated on a project. This one was a summer electronic music workshop held at his Trumansburg factory. The purpose of the workshop was to introduce composers to the modular systems and to get reactions and ideas for technical improvements. Twelve composers attended, many of whom have gone on to direct both university and private studios.

From these beginnings, the interest in small synthesizers spread rapidly. Within a year, the Buchla synthesizer was designed by Donald Buchla, working with composer Morton Subotnik. This was followed by the Electrocomp and shortly thereafter by the ARP, Syn-Ket, and Putney (now known as the Synthi).

Most recently, Japanese and Italian manufacturers have produced synthesizers which, through the use of integrated circuits and some limitations of design, have been made light, small, and portable, as well as quite inexpensive. A most interesting new builder is Roland, a Japanese company presently producing four varieties of small, portable "performance" synthesizers.

MODERN ELECTRONIC MUSIC, PHASE III

By 1966, a handful of Moog Synthesizers (he adopted that name for his systems in that year) had been sold to composers and to two producers of TV jingles. At that time, the Buchla synthesizer was developed on the West Coast, and in the following year an educational project in Connecticut fostered the development of the first Electrocomp (or EML). When, in 1968, the record album *Switched on Bach* made synthesizers a household word, no fewer than six manufacturers were building systems of this sort. As we shall see in later chapters of this book, the synthesizers developed after the first Moog are all quite similar in design and concept.

All produce sound in virtually the same fashion. The electrical signals produced by oscillators are modified by filtering, controlled by keyboards, and shaped by means of envelope generators and voltage-controlled amplifiers. The final output of a synthesizer is a voltage waveform which, when externally amplified and played through a speaker, becomes sound.

At the same time that synthesizers were being developed, engineers and musicians were working together to employ computers in the composition of music. At first, this was aimed at the compositional (structural) process alone, but soon the potential of the computer in the actual synthesis of music became a distinct possibility. A third phase of electronic music had begun.

The first successful computer composition was produced on the Illiac computer at the University of Illinois by Lejaren Hiller. Using a stored "library" of note codes, the computer would continually select these notes at random and compare its selection to a set of "rules" established in order to create a certain style of music. Notes that fit the rules were selected, and notes that did not fit the rules were rejected. The final printout of the work was transcribed into conventional musical notation and performed. The composition (attributed to Hiller, not the computer) was a string quartet called the *Illiac* Suite.

Computer music has more recently taken two basic directions:

1. The use of computers combined with synthesizers, with the computer providing control voltages which can be used to operate different parameters (pitch, timbre, loudness) of the synthesizer
2. The use of computers to determine the actual voltage waveform (direct synthesis)

32

In the first, a computer is programmed to produce a numerical output which is analogous to a DC "control" voltage. In order to transpose the numerical output to a specific voltage, an interfacing device called a digital-to-analog converter must be employed. From the converter, actual voltages are derived which may be directly applied to synthesizers. This type of synthesis is not employed as widely as is direct synthesis of waveforms, but it has been used successfully, notably at the University of Toronto.

In 1958, Max Matthews, director of Behavioral Research at Bell Telephone Laboratories, developed a computer program with which a composer could create any specific waveform mathematically. The numerical series formed is stored as digital information and when the composition is over, the entire digital tape or disc is transposed into magnetic impulses on a standard quarter-inch tape. This process would be accomplished by the use of the same type of digital-to-analog converter. The difference in this approach is that the final magnetic tape could be "played" directly on a tape recorder and the finished composition produced entirely within the computer and converter itself.

Both the beauty and the problem of computer synthesis lie in the responsibilities of the composer. He or she is faced with learning an entirely new and precise vocabulary with which to program every dimension (pitch, duration, timbre, loudness, register) of every single note of any composition. It is a task which many musicians cannot or will not face, and yet it allows total control of a sort dreamed of by the serialists of the early twentieth century.

In the past ten years, a good deal of computer-synthesized composition has taken place. Spearheaded by research in this area at Princeton University, programs of relative clarity have been developed. These are designed to present the programming of computer music with the same type of logic that a composer would apply to operating a synthesizer. The following chart represents the relationship between numerical information and analog waveforms as produced by a computer:

SYNTHESIS

(A) Numerical information as programmed (simplified)

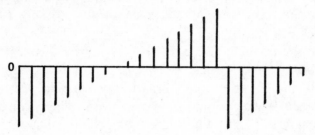

-8, -7, -6, -5, -4, -3, -2, -1, 0, +1, 2, 3, 4, 5, 6, 7, 8, -8, -7, -6, -5, -4, -3, -2, -1

one cycle

(B) Digital representation

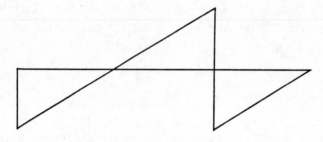

0

(C) Voltage produced by conversion from digital-to-analog

(Each cycle may be repeated as often as required on a periodic basis in order to produce a specific frequency or pitch.)

✓ Computer music has its drawbacks, of course. It has been a difficult area to master, and because of the demands made on the time of most computers large enough to handle music programs, it has become quite expensive. There has been some criticism of computer music because of its "cerebral" quality. (The performer finds it all but impossible to "play" a computer in real time.) Some of the compositions and the research have been very interesting, and the potential of computer synthesis is far greater than that of the synthesizer.

It has been the synthesizer, however, that has attracted the attention of most people to electronic music. Most major

34

universities and colleges are equipped with synthesizer studios, and manufacturers list high schools and even elementary schools as customers. For that reason, the remainder of this book will deal with composition in a synthesizer studio. The instruments discussed in later chapters are those synthesizers most affordable and most widely available in the United States at the time of this writing.

NOTES

1. E. H. Pierce, cited in T. L. Rhea, "The Evolution of Electronic Musical Instruments in the United States" (Ph.D. dissertation, George Peabody College of Teachers, 1972).

2. Herbert Russcol, *The Liberation of Sound* (Englewood Cliffs, N.J.: Prentice-Hall, 1972).

3. The prototype Moog Synthesizer is presently on a semi-permanent loan to Hofstra University, where it is housed as part of the Electronic Music Studio.

3

THE TAPE RECORDER AS
A MUSICAL INSTRUMENT

Although the synthesizer has captured the glory of electronic music, the real workhorse of the field has been the tape recorder. A considerable amount of sound alteration and composition can be accomplished with nothing more than a tape recorder or two, a playback system, some basic skills, and creative imagination. (My own experiences in electronic music began with a SONY 300 tape recorder and a borrowed Ampex. My first successful electronic piece, "Good Friday," was composed in 1962 using chorus, brasses, and tapes. The taped portions were created with only that equipment. Until 1964 I had added only two oscillators and a Theremin to my "studio.")

In this chapter, we will examine these possibilities in a step-by-step manner, beginning with the basic recording process and moving on to the use of a tape recorder as a manipulative instrument. It should be kept in mind that recording is usually the final process in electronic music. The recording of the composition is therefore the "performance" of the work. Just as the performing musician chooses the best available instrument and learns to play it with technical and artistic proficiency, so the electronic music composer should approach the purchase and techniques of the tape recorder.

RECORDING TAPE

Magnetic recording tape consists of a ribbon of *acetate, mylar* or other plastic material upon which a coating of *iron oxide* is applied. The oxide coating is usually a uniform, dull finish, while the plastic backing is shiny. This oxide coating is made up of countless needle-shaped particles which are magnetically aligned in specific patterns corresponding to the electrical waveform during the process of recording. In the playback process, this alignment is used to induce the identical electrical waveforms in the playback head. These become the audio playback. It might be noted that the patterning of the magnetic particles during the recording is somewhat like the compression and rarefaction that will occur in the acoustical transmission as mentioned in Chapter IV.

Commercially available tape is packaged in rolls of various sizes. Most "reel-to-reel" tape recorders within the moderate price range can use reels up to 7 inches in diameter. Professional tape recording is usually done with 10½-inch reels. Both the width and the thickness of recording tape also vary. Quarter-inch tape is used on all low- and moderate-priced tape recorders. Professional recording equipment is designed to handle tape of ½-inch, 1-inch and 2-inch widths. The reason for this is that professional recording is now done on more than two "tracks," and the industrial standard for head design is:

two tracks	¼-inch
four tracks	½-inch
eight tracks	1-inch
sixteen tracks	2-inch

Tape thickness depends upon the thickness of the backing. Standard thicknesses, measured in mils, are 1½m., 1m., and ½m. The thickest tapes, 1½m., are usually available in acetate, polyester, or mylar. Thinner tapes are not made with acetate. The principal advantage of thinner tape is a longer program time, since a 1½m. tape on a 7-inch reel can carry 1200 feet, while ½m. carries 2400 feet. The disadvantages of the thinner tapes are a tendency to *print through*[1] and considerable difficulty in handling and splicing.

It is suggested that *1½m. tape* be used and that composing and experimentation be done with *acetate* tapes, which can be spliced in case of breakage.[2] Master recordings should be transferred to polyester or mylar, which last longer in storage and do not print through as readily.

TAPE-HEAD CONFIGURATION

Cassette tape recorders are not generally used in electronic music since they offer no way to manipulate the recording tape. All recording procedures, head configurations, and so on, will refer to reel-to-reel tape recorders.

In this chapter we will discuss minimal requirements for the electronic music studio tape recorder. The first of these requirements is that it have three heads. The functions of these heads are those of *erase, record,* and *playback.*

The heads on a tape recorder are actually small electromagnetic devices. The erase head discharges any previous magnetic alignment on the tape. The record head, during the *record* mode, magnetizes the particles to represent waveforms, while the playback head, in the playback mode, *reads* these patterns in order to return them to waveform information.

The tape moves from the supply reel to the take-up reel in the following manner:

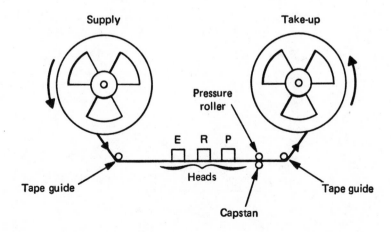

The tape passes first the erase, then the record and playback heads. In the *record* mode, all heads are operating; the erase head demagnetizes any previous recording on the tape, the record head places the new magnetic input onto the erased tape, and the playback head reads the new recording for the purpose of monitoring. In the *playback* mode, the erase and recording heads are turned off.

One of the often confusing areas in head configuration is terminology. We must blame this on inaccurate advertising methods and the use of such terms as "two-track, four-track, quarter-track, half-track, quarter-track mono," and so forth. In truth, this area is quite simple.

Monaural recording is usually done by recording on half of a quarter-inch tape as shown below:

Mono Record Head

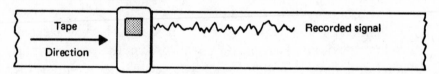

When the recording has been completed, the tape can be taken from the right-hand side of the recorder, turned upside down, and placed as the supply reel. An entirely new "side" can then be recorded. Early "mono" tape recorders recorded on the entire width of the tape. These "full-track" machines are usually found today in AM radio stations where monaural broadcasts are still standard.

Two-track (or half-track) stereo is accomplished by using heads with two separate magnets mounted as follows:

½ — Track Stereo Head

TAPE REVERSAL

In normal recording, when you have completed a stereo tape in half-track, you would not turn over the tape to play the other side since the result would be a backwards playback of the previous recording. In the field of electronic music, the backwards playback of certain sounds can be desirable. Experimentation alone can determine the value of this effect. The performer should note that if the recording had been made in the monaural mode, the backwards playback will be heard over the B channel and the recorded must be played in the stereo mode.

Most tape recorders available for home use are the so-called quarter-track tape recorders. These have become very popular since, although their recording fidelity is slightly inferior to the half-track models, they allow the opportunity of making stereo recordings on "both sides" of a standard tape. The design of a quarter-track stereo head is shown below:

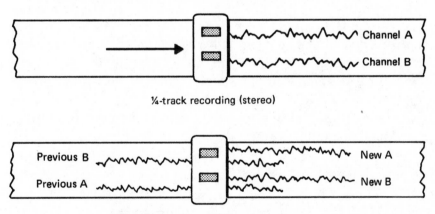

¼-track recording (stereo)

¼-track recording with tape turned over

When using a quarter-track machine and recording monaural, it is possible to obtain four separate recordings on each tape. If this is played on a half-track stereo machine, the resulting sound will be two forward and two backwards tracks. The same effect may be obtained by recording two different stereo programs on a quarter-track stereo recorder and playing the tape on a half-track machine. For the purposes of compositional experimentation, it is advisable to record individual monaural tracks. This will give you greater control over the selected material.

TAPE-SPEED VARIATIONS

Most tape recorders designed for home use operate at two different speeds. In almost all cases these speeds are 3¾-inches per second and 7½-inches per second. Since the speed of the tape movement is proportionate to the amount of tape that passes the heads each second, it should be understood that faster speeds employ more tape (therefore more magnetic surface) and will result in increased recording fidelity. The frequency range that is most affected by speed change is the range of frequencies above 3,000 cycles per second (Hz.). Professional recordings are made at a speed of 15 inches per second, and some fairly expensive home recorders employ this speed.

Tape speed changes can be among the most dramatic effects produced in electronic music. Interesting perceptual effects are created by the variance of pitch, timbre, and tempo as well as by elongation or condensation of spoken words. The speed-change ratio, as you will have noticed is 2:1. Doubling the speed results in doubling all waveform frequencies, and the resulting sound will be heard twice as fast and one octave higher in pitch. The reverse will occur if speed is reduced by half, with the resultant sound an octave lower and half the tempo of the original.

When more than one tape recorder is available, the process of doubling or halving speed can be continued by recording back and forth between the two machines. The following chart is presented as an example of this process:

Step	Tape Recorder #1	Tape Recorder #2	Sound Source	Description
1.	Record at 7½ ips		Four piano notes	Pitch: "c^3," 2048 Hz. Duration of tones: .5 seconds each. Timbre: normal
2.	Playback at 3¾	Record at 7½		
3.	Record at 7½	Playback at 3¾		
4.	Playback at 3¾	Record at 7½		
5.	Record at 7½	Playback at 3¾		Pitch: "C," 128 Hz. Duration of tones: 8 seconds each. Timbre: total change in attack and decay format, hollow tone quality.

Even though many possibilities exist with the speed-change ratio set at 2:1, it can become limiting by its inflexibility after a certain amount of composition time has been spent. Gradual speed changes are even more dramatic and compositionally useful. Some tape recorders have available as optional equipment a device that can vary the speed approximately 25 percent. If professional tape recorders are used, a more efficient and more flexible variable-speed device may be obtained. (In the device referred to, the capstan is driven by a "hysteresis synchronous motor" whose speed is locked to the frequency of an oscillator with frequencies variable from 20 to 80 Hz. For fixed-speed recording, the motor is powered by the standard 60 Hz power lines.) Information of this sort is readily available through the manufacturers' sales representatives.

SPLICING

Since the tape recorder is to be a manipulative musical instrument, considerable thought must be given to *splicing,* the principal manipulation of the tape itself. Interestingly enough, splicing, which would appear to be merely an editing process, can be quite a creative area. Consider the possibilities of the following simple exercise:

> A tone is recorded from a piano, a trumpet, and a flute. In each case the same note (pitch) is played. The attack of the piano is cut off the tape and in its place is spliced the trumpet's attack (without its decay). As the piano tone begins to die away, the end of the flute's note is spliced to it. The result is a traditional musical tone with none of the attack and decay associations of the acoustical instruments that created it.

Splicing is a necessity and must be done in the correct manner for the sake of tape storage as well as musical accuracy. All splicing should be done with a clean sharp razor blade and a professional *splicing block.*

The block should be mounted on the tape recorder if possible and directly below the head assembly. Splicing tape (not ordinary household tape) should always be used. It is advisable to use tape narrower than the recording tape itself. This prevents accidently overlapping the tape, with the glued portion of the splicing tape "bleeding" onto the recording tape during storage. When recording with ¼-inch tape, use 7/32-inch splicing tape.

A splice is made in two steps. It is necessary first to locate and mark the exact area of the splice. This is usually done by ear. With the playback turned on, move the tape manually past the playback head until the area to be spliced is found. Remember that the sound is located on the tape directly at the center of the playback head. Mark the tape either at that point (being careful not to mark the head itself) or at some other point which can be measured on both the recorder and the splicing block.

The second step of splicing is of course the cutting and taping of the spliced parts. Use the center of the diagonal cutting groove to coincide with the splicing mark. When the cuts have been made, take a small piece of splicing tape (about an inch) and, using the flat section of the razor blade, place it over the butted ends of the recording tape.

A carefully butted, diagonally cut, *clean* splice will *not* be heard during playback.

Diagram of Spliced Tape on Splicing Block

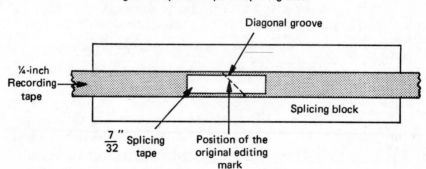

TAPE LOOPS

The *tape loop* is one of the classic techniques of electronic music. Simple and effective, it is employed to produce various ostinato patterns. The procedure is a simple one. A recording is made which the performer desires to repeat for the purposes of rhythm, pitch, intensity, and dramatic quality. The starting and ending points are determined, and the tape marked, cut, and spliced to itself to form a closed loop. There are infinite possibilities for tape loop variations, but some guidelines may be followed. Short, percussive sounds produce very exciting loops because of the rhythmic possibilities. Unusual juxtapositions of sound can be very effective in a loop. Words and vocal sounds make very dramatic tape loops. Sustained instrumental or vocal sounds are less effective, since performance variations will be quite noticeable at the splice.

The playback of a tape loop requires some attention. In order to be played without distortion, the normal tension must be maintained in the threading of the tape on the recorder. This will require using the tape tension arm and, depending upon the length of the loop, a possible external guide around which the tape will pass. The following diagrams show two possible setups for the playback of tape loops:

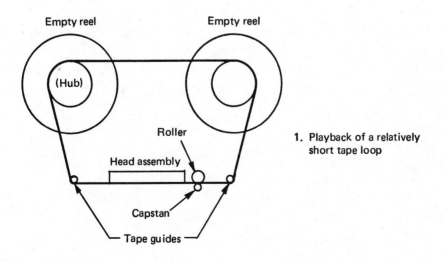

1. Playback of a relatively short tape loop

45

2. Playback of longer tape loop using a microphone stand

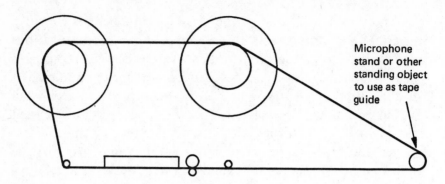

Microphone stand or other standing object to use as tape guide

SOUND-ON-SOUND

All electronic music composition requires some degree of *multi-tracking*. What this means in essence is the addition of sounds to a recording while monitoring whatever has been previously recorded. On sophisticated studio equipment this is done with recording heads that are divided into 4, 8, or 16 separate magnets or "channels." Each "track" of the composition is recorded and played back by use of a separate amplifier. Any channel of the head can be played by itself or with others in any combination and in either a *record,* a *playback,* or a *synchronized* mode.

Tape recorders designed for commercial studio work are, without a doubt, the best equipment to use for electronic music. They are also far more expensive than the home tape recorder. Before we discuss these machines, therefore, it would be best to examine the smaller and less expensive tape recorder, which is equipped with a special type of multi-track function called *sound-on-sound.*

Again it is important to repeat that your tape recorder must have three separate heads for erase, record, and playback. If it does, and it is a stereo machine, it should also have the sound-on-sound function built in. In its simplest sense, sound-on-sound can be explained as follows:

46

1. A recording is made on track A.
2. Track A is played back (and monitored) while being simultaneously mixed with a *new* signal being recorded onto track B. The result is that *both* will now appear on track B.
3. Track B is played back (and monitored) while being simultaneously mixed with a *new* signal being recorded onto Track A. The result is that now all *three* will appear on track A.
4. The process is repeated until all desired parts have been recorded.

A block diagram for the sound-on-sound process would appear as follows:

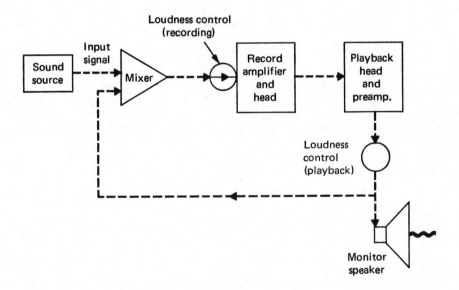

It can be seen on the diagram that the playback loudness control will allow the performer to determine the amount of the first recording to be mixed with the second recording, while the recording loudness control will become a master for each new recording.

What is *not* shown on the diagram for reasons of clarity is that in order to employ sound-on-sound, *the input signal must be switched from one channel to the other at each recording.* Since there is a physical distance of an inch or two between the record and playback heads, the recording on the tape might be represented in the following manner:

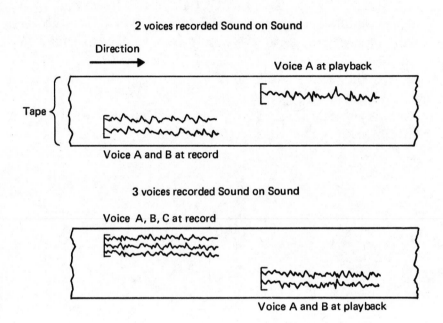

2 voices recorded Sound on Sound

Direction

Voice A at playback

Tape

Voice A and B at record

3 voices recorded Sound on Sound

Voice A, B, C at record

Voice A and B at playback

The unusual effect (usually unintentional) of having one voice appear a split second behind the next will result if the final recording is played back in the "stereo" mode.

SIGNAL-TO-NOISE RATIO

If a recording with, let's say, six separate voices is made, using sound-on-sound, it should be obvious that the first voice to be recorded will have been rerecorded five more times before the piece is completed. Each *generation* (recording process) will add a certain amount of normal amplifier and tape noise to the signal. In the case of most home tape recorders, this noise is quite audible after three or four generations. This does not make sound-on-sound recording impossible, but it presents a problem that must be solved by careful choice of tape recorder and by care in the recording process.

A certain amount of ambient noise is produced by all amplifiers and by recording tapes, and will be recorded with the signal. Obviously, the relationship between the desired signal and the undesired noise must be considered. This relationship, called the *signal-to-noise ratio,* is measured by the engineers who designed the tape recorder. It is, therefore, available in the manufacturer's specifications. Signal-to-noise ratios are measured in *decibels,* the standard measurement of loudness. One number is given, which represents the loudness, in *db,* of the signal above the noise. High signal-to-noise ratios are therefore desirable. When choosing a tape recorder, look for a signal-to-noise ratio of at least 55 db, based on a recording level that produces no more than 3 percent harmonic distortion.

When making a sound-on-sound recording, always record the first signal at maximum loudness (with least distortion). This will assure a strong recording which will not be "lost" in subsequent generations. (A general recording rule is to make most recordings at a high level. Levels can always be reduced, while signal-to-noise remains unchanged.)

The loudness level of a recording is measured by a VU (for volume unit) meter. It is important that there be a separate *VU meter* for each channel on the tape recorder selected for an electronic music studio. The standard VU meter is calibrated in db above and below the recorder's *maximum* permissible recording level. There is usually an additional calibration representing the percentage of recordable signal from 0 (no audible signal) to 100 percent (maximum before possible distortion). A VU meter should never be "pinned" (the needle going to the far right), since that is likely to result in a distorted recording. It is best to record the *highest* portions of your signal with the needle slightly into "the red" in order to maintain high signal-to-noise ratios. A standard VU scale is shown below:

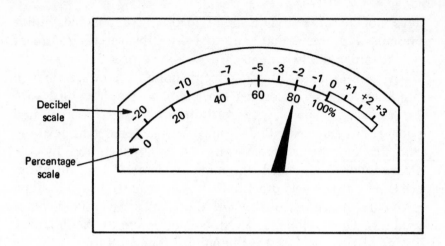

TAPE-HEAD ECHO

Echo effects are very common and, if not overdone, are valuable in electronic music. These effects can be produced on any recorder which uses three heads to produce sound-on-sound. The procedure consists simply of using the playback head to *feed back* a portion of the recording to the record head and record it over again, continuing the process until the sound becomes inaudible. On a professional tape recorder this can be done easily, since the playback head can be turned on during the recording process. All that is needed is a mixer into which both the sound source and the playback signal are fed. The block diagram for this technique can be represented as follows:

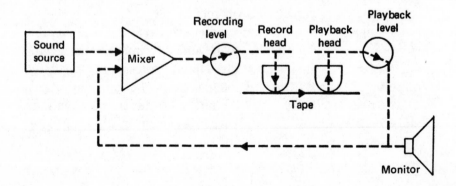

50

The recording level will control the loudness of the recording while the playback level will control the strength and number of repetitions of the event.

The echo effect is created by the distance between the record and playback heads. Needless to say, tape speed and the actual distance between the heads determine the time between echoes.

Many home tape recorders are available with the echo function. On these machines, the manufacturer's instructions will explain the procedure. It is important to study them carefully, because virtually every make of tape recorder uses different terminology for what is basically the same function.

Since potentially the same circuitry which achieves sound-on-sound can also be used for echo, the designers of smaller recorders have usually built in an *echo loop* that, like sound-on-sound, employs both channels. The result is a *stereophonic echo* which can be a very interesting spatial effect in playback. In this procedure, the recording is made on track A and played back immediately. The playback is sent directly to track B where it is recorded and played back immediately. It is then sent back to track A, and the procedure continues. A block diagram of this echo loop (sometimes called a *feedback loop*) follows:

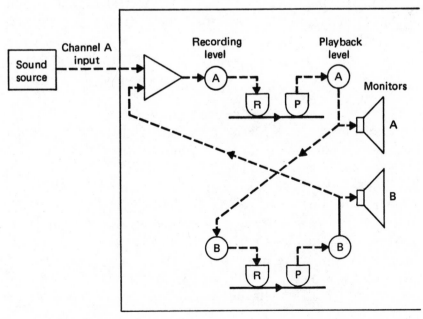

It is impossible for an echo loop to produce an echo signal that does not either increase or decrease in amplitude. If the echoes become increasingly stronger than the original signal, the result will become a loud "wail" which will eventually damage the speakers if played at a high volume. Echoes which *increase* in loudness are products of *positive feedback*. *Negative feedback* is the production of echoes lower in amplitude than the original signal. This is the standard form of echo effect heard in electronic music.

TAPE STUDIO SETUP

As we have seen, the tape recorders chosen for an electronic music studio must be stereophonic, three-head machines capable of both sound-on-sound and echo. It is also advisable that a tape recorder have *three separate motors,* one for capstan drive, one for take-up drive, and one for supply (rewind). The *capstan* motor is the critical one, because the capstan speed will determine the amount of undesired motion ("wow" and "flutter") that occurs in the tape drive. It is imperative for pitch accuracy that the capstan motor either be a hysteresis synchronous motor or be driven by some other controlled-speed method. Having separate motors for the take-up and rewind reduces the number of mechanical parts (pulleys or belts) in the transport itself and assures longer periods without maintenance. This is especially important for machines handled by many different people, or started and stopped often, as in an electronic music studio.

Quadraphonic recording equipment using ¼-inch tape is now readily available. This makes many studio conveniences such as "in-line" multi-track recording available at much lower prices than ever before. The advantage of a four-channel tape recorder is that each track can be recorded separately with a four-part composition having all first-generation recordings. In order to synchronize this recording, an electronic circuit is added which enables the channels of the recording head to be switched individually to playback. It is possible in this manner to record a signal on channel A, switch channel A to the *Sync mode* and record on channel B while hearing the playback of A

52

at the *same* position on the tape that B is being recorded. This device is called *selective synchronization* and is generally known by the Ampex trademark *sel-sync.* For electronic music purposes, purchase of a quadraphonic tape recorder without sel-sync would be pointless.

When setting up the recording portion of a studio, it is advisable to obtain a mixer. There are many available at moderate cost, and most are suitable for recording purposes. The principal qualifications for the studio mixer should be:

1. At least four input channels
2. At least two output channels
3. Microphone preamplifiers on at least two channels
4. Line output correctly matching the input impedance of the tape recorder
5. Headphone monitor jack

Once a studio has a relatively permanent location, all of the equipment should be connected to a *patch panel.* This is a device you can easily make, since it consists only of a number of jacks which are connected to the inputs and outputs of all studio components. The patch panel allows the performer to interconnect tape recorder, mixer, synthesizer, and other equipment without the confusion of wires running every which way and without leaving one work area. The mixer and patch panel become the "control console" for the studio. The most convenient size of plug and jack to use is the ¼-inch phone jack. This is large enough to handle with ease, is readily available at all electronic supply stores, and is easy to solder and use for making *patch cords.* These cords have a ¼-inch phone plug at each end and should be about two feet long. With the patch panel, they are used to provide the interconnections as shown below:

	Mixer				Tape		Tape		Synthesizer			Amp	
In O	O	O	O	O	O		O	O	O	O	O	O	In
	A	B	C	D	A	B	A	B	A	B	C		
Out O	O	O	O	O	O		O	O	O	O	O	O	Out

Patch Panel — Sample Front View

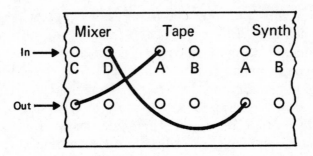

Patch going from synthesizer to mixer, from mixer to tape

SPATIAL SOUND "LOCATION"

The perception of spatial movement and depth, as briefly mentioned in chapter III, is created in electronic music by the use of multiple amplifiers, speakers and recorded tracks. When two tracks are used, along with two amplifiers and speakers, the result is stereophony, or stereo sound. The use of four tracks, amplifiers, and speakers is referred to as quadraphonic sound, or quad.

When employing multiple channels of sound in playback, it is possible to create distinctly separate sound points by having different sound sources appear at each speaker. It is also possible to create illusions of depth by mixing all sounds while still emphasizing certain sound sources at each speaker. This provides a more realistic playback and is used in the making of commercial recordings.

The movement of sound in space is obtained by a technique known as *panning*. (The term is borrowed from the motion picture technique of moving a camera slowly across a scene.) In panning from one speaker to another, the sound to be panned is sent primarily into one channel during the final mix. As this recording continues, the amplitude of the sound into that channel is *decreased* while it is slowly and proportionately *increased* into a second channel. In playback, this sound will appear to move across the room between the speakers.

Although considerable practice is required to perfect panning and the placement of sound locations, these techniques are widely used and are valuable to the composer, especially with the availability of inexpensive quad recorders and playback systems.

MICROPHONES

An important decision in setting up the studio will be the choice of microphones. It is suggested that either *dynamic* or *condenser* microphones be used in electronic music applications. Dynamic microphones are less expensive and generally not capable of frequency response as wide as that of condenser microphones. The dynamic microphone operates on a principle that may be likened to the reverse of a loudspeaker. A diaphragm is moved by the sound wave, and it is attached to a small coil which moves within the field of a permanent magnet to produce electrical representations of the acoustical waveform. Condenser microphones generate electrical signals by varying capacitance between the electrically charged diaphragm plate and a second charged plate. The resultant signal voltage is then amplified before being used as the recording signal.

The most important specifications for a microphone are its *frequency response, impedance,* and *pattern.* The frequency response states the lowest and highest frequencies to be transmitted by the microphone. It is very important that a printed *response curve* be available, since the area of *flat response* (those frequencies between which there is little or no amplitude deviation) is often more critical than the stated frequency response. For example, the following diagram represents the response curve of a hypothetical microphone which claims a frequency response of 40-12 KHz., but which would obviously not be suitable for the recording of bass instruments since its amplitude has fallen off sharply below 700 Hz.:

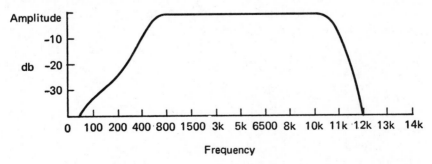

Microphones are available with either high- or low-output impedance. The advantage of low over high is that there is less chance of electrical interference caused by improper shielding and less chance of high frequency loss due to long microphone lines. There is also a slightly larger selection of professional equipment available with only low impedance outputs. Most home tape recorders are designed for high impedance microphones, however, so it is best to check this before purchasing the microphones.

All microphones do not record with the same pattern. Some pick up from all directions, others only from the front, others from front and back. The following diagram represents the standard microphone patterns:

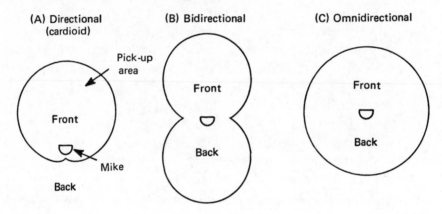

In the diagrams, the greater distances from the microphones represent the greater areas of sensitivity to pickup.

CONCLUSION

The tape recorder is the basic instrument in the creation of electronic music. All procedures discussed in this chapter should be learned, since skill with the recorder will not only be important in the composition of tape music, but it will also add immeasurably to success with the synthesizer. Spend as much time as possible with the recording studio alone, using as many procedures as you can to compose sound collages, random mixes, and structured compositions.

56

NOTES

1. Print-through is the effect created when the magnetic signal transfers to the adjoining layer of tape when rolled up on the reel. Commercial studios store their tapes on the take-up reel ("tails out") so that the print-through occurs after the initial sound and is usually masked and unnoticed.

2. In case of a handling error, mylar or polyester tapes usually will not break, but will stretch, thereby distorting the recording.

TERMINOLOGY FOR STUDY

Before going on to "In the Studio," it is very important that you understand the following terms. Be able to define them in your own words.

acetate	generation
mylar	VU meter
iron oxide	feedback loop
1½ mil, 1 mil, ½ mil	stereo echo
print through	positive feedback
erase, record, playback	negative feedback
monaural	capstan
splicing block	sel-sync
tape loop	patch panel
multi-track	microphone response curve
sound-on-sound	cardioid
signal-to-noise ratio	omnidirectional

4

THE ELECTRONIC SYNTHESIS OF SOUND

BASICS

Three elements are needed if sound is to exist:

1. *Generation.* Without some sort of physical vibrations (called oscillatory motion), there can be no starting point to the phenomenon of sound.
2. *Transmission.* These vibrations (oscillations) are transmitted by the *compression* and *rarefaction* of molecules within some *conductive* material (usually air, but water and many solids also can conduct sound waves).
3. *Perception.* The eardrum and related bone structures of the ear are set in motion in proportion to the transmitted waves. This motion, interpreted as electrochemical messages, is sent to the brain and, depending upon familiarity and education, is understood as a particular sound.

Musicians today often refer to the existence of two groups of instruments: those that are either electronic or dependent upon amplification, and those that are traditionally designed and/or not dependent upon amplification. These are popularly called either "electric" or "acoustic" instruments. Not very accurate terminology, but usable.

In traditional "acoustic" instruments, the vibrations (or

59

oscillations) are produced by some direct physical force: the drawing of a bow across a stretched string, the hitting or plucking of a string, the vibration of a player's tightly held lips, the blowing of air through a reed, etc. These vibrations are transferred to back-and-forth movements of the air molecules by the physical design of the instrument. The back-and-forth molecular vibrations are the compression and rarefaction that, traveling from the instrument in waves, represent the transmission of the sound.

Consider, as an example, the operation of a string instrument such as the violin.

When the player draws a bow across the string, the string is set into motion. The speed of this vibrating motion is called *frequency* and is measured in the number of complete vibration cycles that take place in one second. This frequency differs in proportion to certain variables. On a violin, the most common of these variables determining frequency are the thickness and texture of the strings (heavy strings vibrate more slowly) and the position of the fingers of the player on the fingerboard (shortening the string length by pressing down fingers makes the string vibrate faster). The player's choice of which string to draw the bow across and which finger to press at a point on the fingerboard may be referred to as the *frequency control* factors of violin playing.

Impedance is the property of any substance or device which impedes or appears to resist vibrations. In order to have the most effective transmission of vibrations from one body to another, it is necessary that the impedances of the two bodies be "matched." Horns, tubes, sounding boards, and resonators such as violin bodies serve to match the very high impedance of the original physical vibrating bodies with the low impedance of air.

When the violin string is set in motion, the sound that it produces is almost indiscernible. These vibrations, however, are carried from the strings through the bridge and into the body of the violin which is an almost sealed wooden resonator. In the violin's body the *impedances* are matched and the vibrations are transferred to the air where, traveling as waves, they radiate in all directions from the instrument.

60

The sound waves are transmitted through the air as proportionate compressions and rarefactions of air molecules. As the distance from the sound source to the *perceiver* becomes greater, the adjustment of the molecules becomes affected by a gradual dispersion of the vibrating energy, and the loudness and clarity of the sound is eventually lost.

The following chart represents the *generation* and *transmission* of a sound as produced by a violin.

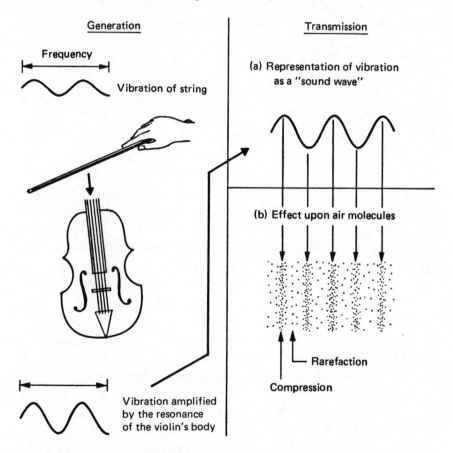

One of the most important factors in the *perception* of sound is the environment of the perceiver. Room size and design, atmospheric conditions, even the position of the listener in relation to the sound source, will effect perception.

The perceptual mechanism of the human being is so accurate that the time factor in the reception of a moving

61

sound source will be considered by the brain in determining the position of the sound. If the listener sits perfectly still and a sound moves from side to side before him, the waves will naturally reach each ear at a different time. The brain will correctly interpret that time difference as a perception of movement. In stereophonic and quadraphonic sound systems, that time differential is produced through the placement of multiple sound sources (speakers).

A considerable amount of electronic music has been composed with the spatial effects of speaker placement considered by the composer to be an integral part of the composition itself. One of the first, and most notable, was *Poème Electronique* by Edgard Varèse, composed for the Philips Pavilion of the Brussels Worlds Fair in 1957. Its performance was swept through 400 speakers of a specially designed building, and it became one of the high points of the fair's attractions.

The environments of rooms differ considerably in their acoustic properties. The determinants of room acoustics are the amounts of *echo* or *reverberation* perceived along with the original sound. Since sound waves travel in all directions, some of these will be perceived directly by the listener, while others will bounce off the walls and ceilings and return at varying times as echoes of the original sound. Echoes occurring after a sound is heard are easily produced by electro-mechanical means with a tape recorder. In nature, they seldom occur unless there is a large space between the sound source, the perceiver, and the point from which the echo bounces. This type of echo traditionally occurs in mountains or ravines.

Reverberation, when the individual echoes come so close on each other that they blend together, is a common factor in all rooms. It exists so much in the concert hall environment of traditional music, in fact, that artificial (electronic) reverberation is frequently added to recordings in order to create a realistic effect. Acoustical reverberation is produced when sound waves are reflected from the many different objects in a room (walls, floors, ceilings, furniture) and perceived with numerous minute time differences by the listener. The effects of reverberation range from "warmth" (slight reverberation present) to "muddiness" (too much reverberation present).

In the electronic synthesis of sound, generation, in the traditional sense, begins with the movement of the cone of a loudspeaker. *It is the function of an electronic music synthesizer to initiate this process.* In later chapters, we will discuss the synthesizer and the various components of electronic music studios. Before that, some of the more basic concepts of *electroacoustics* should be understood. For the sake of clarity, we will begin with . . .

THE LOUDSPEAKER

The loudspeaker is one of a class of devices, called *transducers,* used in all electrical sound synthesis and recording. A transducer changes one sort of energy into another. The speaker changes electrical energy into physical vibrations, and the microphone (another common transducer) changes physical vibrations into electrical energy. Phonograph pickups (cartridges) and tape recorder heads are also transducers.

Most speakers operate on a very simple principle. They consist of a paper cone suspended in a rigid frame. Attached to the center of the cone is a coil of fine wire. The unit is designed so that if the coil were to move back and forth, the cone would move along with it:

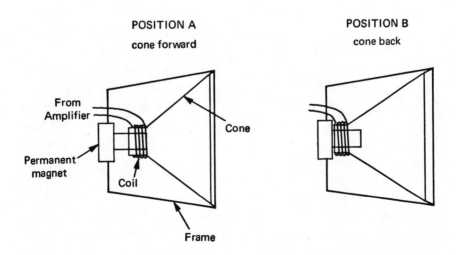

POSITION A
cone forward

POSITION B
cone back

From Amplifier

Cone

Permanent magnet

Coil

Frame

63

Attached to the rear of the speaker frame is a permanent magnet. The coil attached to the cone is connected to a source of electrical current from an amplifier. As the current alternates, an alternating force is produced between the coil and the magnet. This causes the cone to move back and forth according to the shape of the aforementioned waveform. *The movement of the speaker cone, therefore, is directly proportionate to the shape of the waveform.*

The *frequency* of the waveform determines the number of complete cycles per second (back and forth movements) made by the speaker cone. This in turn determines the frequency of the compression and rarefaction caused by the cone's movement and will relate to the "pitch" perceived by the listener. The *amplitude* of the waveform determines the energy of this back and forth movement. It will determine the distance the molecules actually move, and will relate to the perception of loudness.

OSCILLATORS AND WAVEFORMS

Since acoustical generation of electronic music begins with the loudspeaker, the composer is actually involved with determining, shaping, and controlling a waveform. An *oscillator* generally begins the process.

An oscillator is a device that produces an alternating electrical current. This current is represented by a specific waveform and is generated at a frequency determined by some physical control device. The frequency range of oscillators used in electronic music is from 1 cycle every five seconds to 20,000 cycles per second. Within the past few years, the term Hertz (Hz. after Heinrich Hertz, a nineteenth-century German physicist) has come to replace "cycles per second." An *audio frequency oscillator* is one that produces oscillations between the frequencies of 20 and 20,000 Hz., which is the range of human hearing. The use of frequencies below the audio range (subaudio frequencies) is also important in electronic music and will be discussed in later chapters.

The frequency range of an oscillator can be controlled

either manually or automatically. Manual control is made by adjusting a *potentiometer* on the oscillator itself. A potentiometer is a specially connected variable resistor and is used for many different controls in audio and electronic music. (For example, on a radio or TV receiver, the loudness control is a potentiometer.) When an oscillator is controlled automatically, its frequency responds to differing *control voltages.* Both types of control will be found in electronic music syntehsizers. Automatic control by control voltage also will be discussed in detail in later chapters.

The "height" of a waveform is its *amplitude,* measured in voltage above and below the zero point. Amplitude, when applied to the function of a speaker, will determine the loudness of the sound produced by the waveform of the oscillator. The following diagram represents the *output* of a sine wave oscillator:

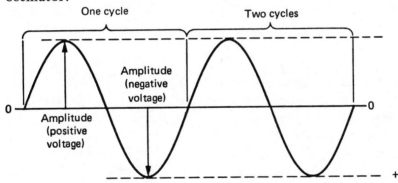

The term *complex waveform* refers technically to any waveform other than the sine wave. All other waveforms represent the addition of other frequencies to the fundamental frequency as represented by a sine wave. Almost all sounds are made up of complex waveforms. Most musical instruments produce sounds with their frequency components in a specific ratio to the fundamental frequency. The ratio is in whole-number multiples of the fundamental and is called *harmonic ratio.* The tones in harmonic ratio to a fundamental are referred to as *overtones* or *harmonics.*

As an example of waveform synthesis, imagine four sine wave oscillators. One is tuned to a frequency of 100 Hz., the

65

second to 300 Hz., the third to 500 Hz., and the fourth to 700 Hz. If the amplitudes of each are arranged in such a manner that the fundamental (the lowest frequency) is the loudest, while the next three are proportionately softer, they can be represented separately in the following illustration:

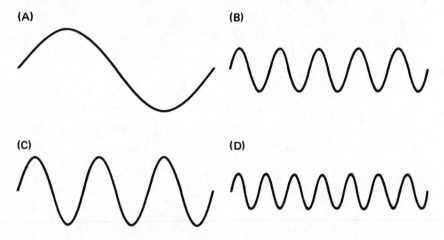

The frequencies chosen represent the fundamental, third, fifth, and seventh harmonic from the frequency 100 Hz. When *mixed* together, all four waveforms will produce a complex waveform as represented below:

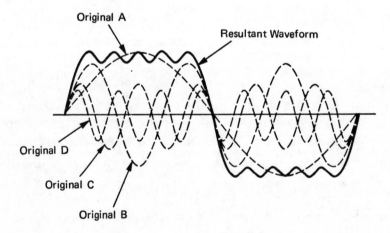

The waveform designated in the diagram as the *resultant wave-form* is the only one that now exists, and *it has within it all of the characteristics of each of its parts.*

66

The scientists Helmholtz and Fourier have proved mathematically that waveforms, no matter how complex, may be resolved into individual (harmonic) frequency components....[1]

Since, in the example above, the 100 Hz. sine wave has the lowest frequency and the highest amplitude, it becomes the determinant of the *pitch* while the other sine waves become determinants of the *timbre*.

The composers of electronic music during the 1950s often synthesized all of their complex waveforms by employing banks of dozens of sine-wave oscillators. If, for instance, three or four more sine-wave oscillators were available for the example above, and were tuned to continue the obvious mathematical progression already begun as 1, 3, 5, 7, the result would be a waveform almost *square*. The following chart represents the use of eight sine-wave oscillators used to synthesize a square wave:

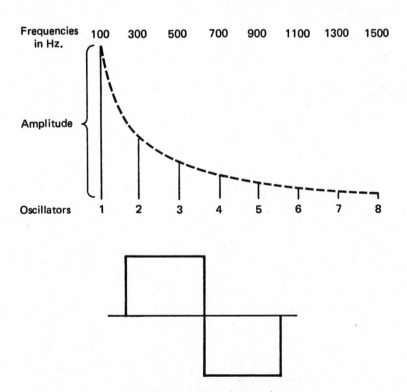

Resultant waveform (approx.)

By employing eight or more sine-wave oscillators carefully set at frequencies representing the odd-numbered harmonics, and with their amplitudes dropping off from the fundamental as shown, a *square wave,* sounding very much like a clarinet in its low register, could be electronically synthesized.

On the modern synthesizers, this procedure is unnecessary. All oscillators on today's instruments are multi-functional and have anywhere from two to six *different* waveforms available at the flick of a switch. The following waveforms are generated by the oscillators of most synthesizers:

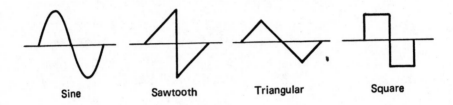

| Sine | Sawtooth | Triangular | Square |

In later chapters, waveforms and their characteristic timbres will be discussed. Remember that the *shape* of the waveform will determine the manner in which the speaker cone moves, and ultimately will determine the timbre of the tones.

AMPLIFIERS

As we have seen, the output of an oscillator is an alternating current with a definable frequency and amplitude. The amplitude of the waveform is measured in *voltage.* Its energy, when it leaves the oscillator, is ordinarily not strong enough to operate a speaker. At this point, an additional step is needed between the generation of the waveform and the acoustical generation. This will enable the waveform to retain its shape and frequency, but will greatly increase its amplitude. The step is called *amplification.*

An amplifier is a device that accepts an *input* of any shape and frequency of waveform. Its function is to sample this waveform, and feed it back into a circuit of much higher current. In this circuit, called an *amplification stage,* the higher current takes on the characteristics of the original input. This process is usually repeated through several stages until the amplification has achieved sufficient power to drive the speakers. *The essential point in amplification is that the input is minute, while the output is large!*

The *fidelity* of an amplifier refers to its ability to accomplish this increase in power without destroying any other elements of the input waveform (i.e., the frequency or shape). *Distortion* refers to the alteration of the original waveform by the amplifier. The diagrams below show a hypothetical input signal amplified with high fidelity (A) and with distortion (B) in loud portions.

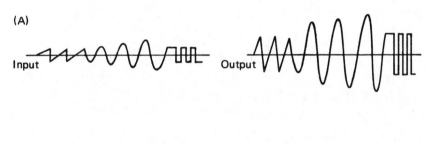

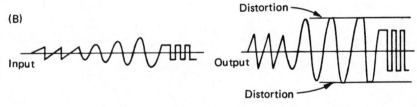

In the second example, the loudest points have been distorted in a typical manner. Unable to maintain the characteristic shape at highest amplitudes, the amplifier has "clipped" or cut off the high and low peaks at those points, thereby changing the waveform and adding sounds characteristic of that new shape.

In the diagram below, a sound is created. Note that two stages are represented: the electronic synthesis, and the acoustical stage.

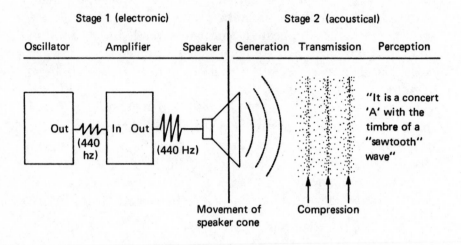

CONCLUSION

In electronic music, the acoustical phenomenon of sound begins with the loudspeaker. It is the function of synthesizers to create electrical waveforms that will activate loudspeakers. These waveforms are usually generated by oscillators, but must be amplified before they have the energy to drive a speaker. When this rather simple process is clearly understood, the following chapters, dealing with the complete functions of the synthesizers, will not be difficult.

NOTES

1. F. C. Judd, *Electronic Music and Musique Concrète* (London: Neville Spearman, 1961), p. 19.

TERMINOLOGY FOR STUDY

Before going on to the next chapters, it is very important that you understand the following terms. Be able to define them in your own words.

generation	speaker cone	complex waveform
transmission	oscillator	cycle
perception	audio frequency	amplitude
frequency	potentiometer	voltage
sound waves	waveform	input and output
echo	harmonics	fidelity
reverberation	impedance	distortion
transducer	fundamental	

Herbert A. Deutsch, in 1964, working on the development of the Moog Synthesizer.
(Photographed by Robert Moog)

Robert A. Moog (left) and Herbert A. Deutsch operating the original Moog Synthesizer prototype, currently housed at Hofstra University.

Live electronic music — Herbert A. Deutsch (right) with "The Kitchen Sync" in concert. Greg Dib, audio engineer, and Frank Stratton are shown. Drummer Jim Pirone is not shown.

Walter Carlos in his studio with an elaborate Moog Synthesizer.

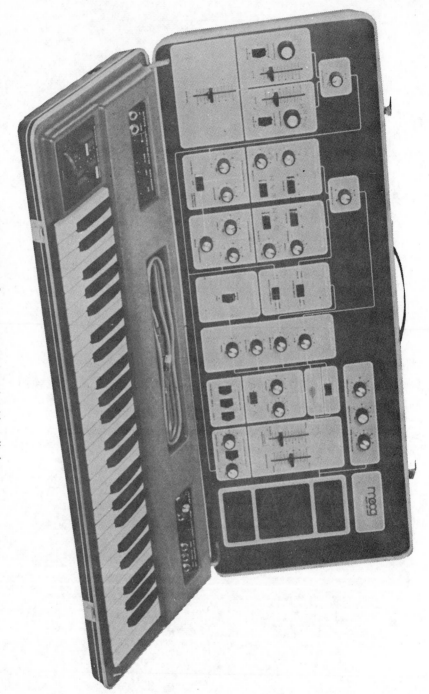

Moog "Sonic ⅥΙ" — designed for school installations.

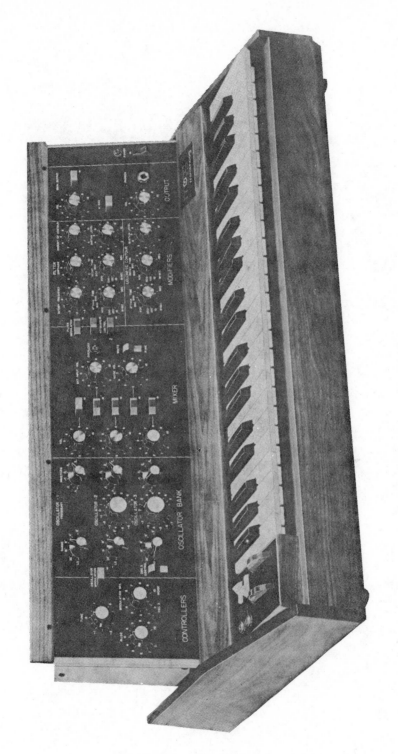

The Minimoog — a very popular small synthesizer.

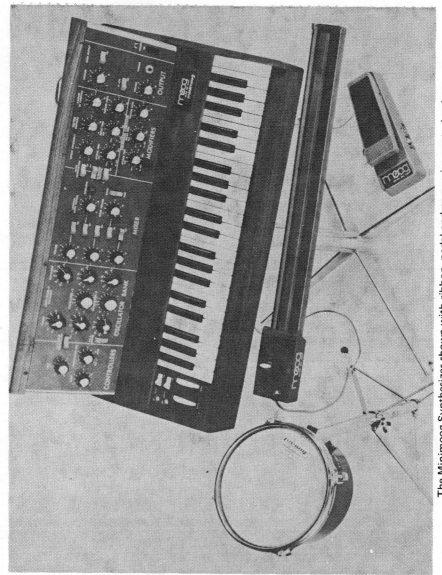

The Minimoog Synthesizer shown with ribbon, pedal and percussive control units.

Moog "Satellite" — a small preset performance synthesizer.

Moog "Model 12" — a single unit designed for patch-cord interconnection.
Contains all standard modules of the small synthesizers.
(Keyboard not shown)

ARP "pro soloist" — a small preset performance synthesizer.

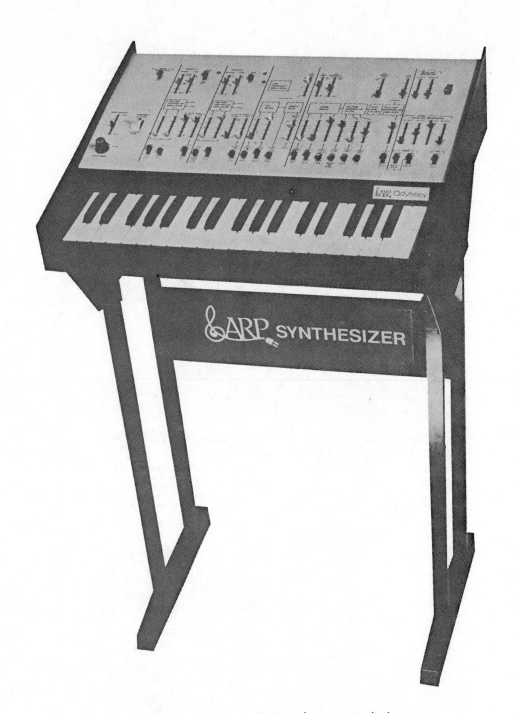

ARP "Odyssey" — a small, completely controllable performance synthesizer.

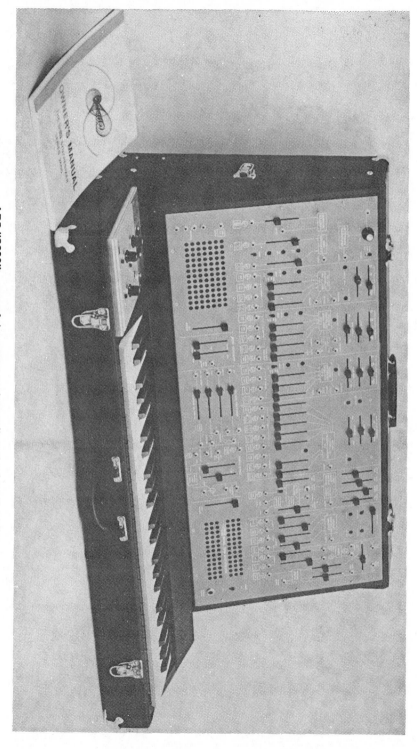

ARP "2600" — one of the most popular medium sized synthesizers.

Large ARP studio system.

SYNTHI — a complete small synthesizer built into an attaché case.

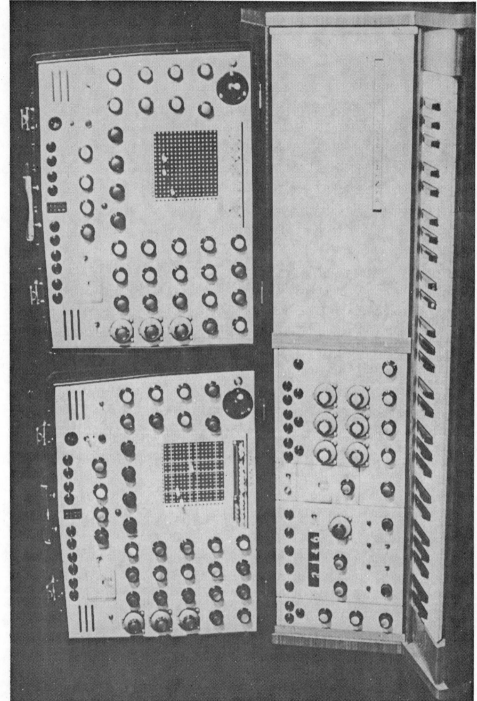

An electronic music system consisting of two SYNTHI units above a digital sequencer with keyboard control.

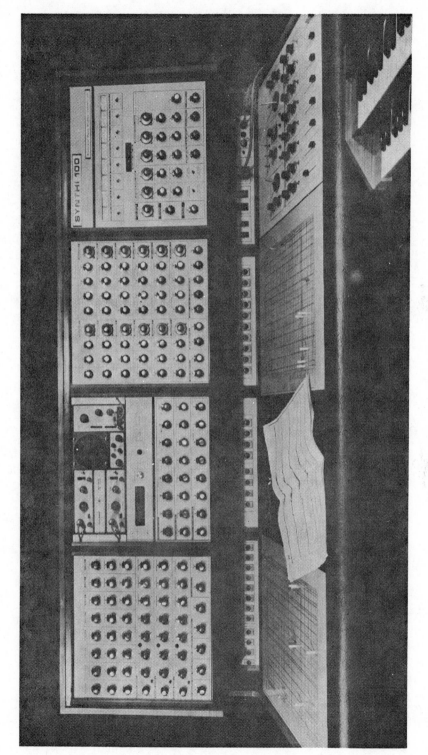

SYNTHI 100 — a large studio synthesizer system.

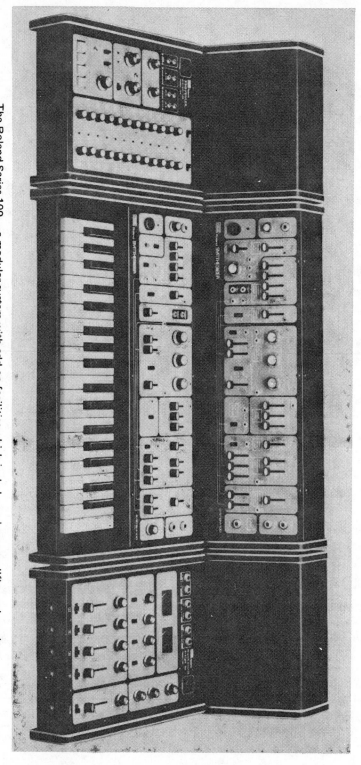

The Roland Series 100 — a modular system with add-on facilities which include a mixer, amplifier and speakers.

5

ELECTRONIC MUSIC SYNTHESIZERS (1)

All of the electronic music synthesizers made since the first Moog in 1964 have two important things in common: (1) they are modularly conceived and (2) they employ the concept of voltage control.

The concept of modules is that you do not have to think of the synthesizer as one huge complex circuit. Instead, it is conceived as an interconnected group of fairly simple circuits, or *functional modules.* Each individual module is easy to understand and has its own special purpose.

Voltage control means that the functions of these modular components, whether oscillators, amplifiers, or filters, can in some way be modified and controlled by a measurable amount of dc voltage. *Control voltages,* as they are called, can be used to change an oscillator's pitch, increase or decrease an amplitude, modify timbre, or combine any or all of these functions simultaneously. The performer on an electronic music synthesizer almost always operates some type of control voltage, and most frequently with a keyboard, the common source of control voltages.

The amount of control voltage used in any module of the synthesizer is directly *analogous* to the output of that module. This is true if the module referred to produces pitches, controls loudness, or changes timbre. This proportion (or analogy) between control and output makes the electronic music synthesizer an *analog device.*

Larger analog devices are used by industry in numerous ways. Industrial automation employs analog computer systems which use control voltages directly to operate machinery.

All synthesizers are made up of four basic categories of modules, according to their functions:

1. Signal generators
2. Signal modifiers
3. Controllers
4. Mixers

A *signal* is the term used to describe that electrical flow which will eventually become heard as sound. Some manufacturers refer (somewhat inaccurately) to signal generators as "sound" generators. A simple flow chart can best describe the synthesizer in its basic form.

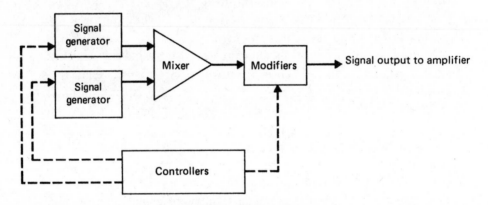

AUDIO OSCILLATORS

Signal generators consist of oscillators and random generators. Audio oscillators are those devices which produce frequencies within the range of human hearing. All synthesizers have approximately the same audio oscillators, although there are differences in the waveform availabilities and the identifying terminology. The pitches produced may be varied by two controls directly on the oscillator panel. One is a coarse control, usually calibrated in octaves. The other is a fine or vernier control. This is a potentiometer which provides a gliding pitch change over a distance of about one or two octaves. Since the audio oscillators are voltage-controlled, these two controls are actually ways in which the performer can manually "set" a certain amount of control voltage. There is also a variable position switch which determines the output waveform to be selected, and on some synthesizers a control to vary the width of a pulse wave, if that is the chosen output form.

CONTROL SYSTEMS

Besides setting a fixed control on the panel of the oscillator, there are other ways of providing control voltages to the audio oscillators. The most common device is the keyboard. Synthesizer keyboards are simply variable voltage sources. When a key is depressed, a switch is thrown, sending a given amount of dc voltage to the control portion of the oscillator. This in turn sets the frequency at a specific point, thereby producing a note. We can represent the keyboard as a basic source of voltages with each key acting as a resistance, thereby changing that voltage according to the patterns of "tempered tuning." When a voltage-controlled oscillator is so designed that a one-volt change in control voltage will represent a doubling in frequency (one octave), the following diagram would represent the keyboard and its relationship to the oscillator:

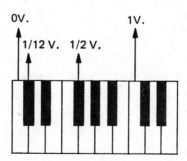

Keeping in mind what we have already noted about the coarse and fine adjustments on the panel of the oscillators themselves, we can arrive at an interesting observation. Middle C, for example, can be tuned the same as its piano counterpart by depressing that note and adjusting the coarse and fine adjustments until the oscillator is in tune. From that point on, the entire keyboard will remain proportionately the same as the keyboard of a piano. Of course it is always possible to change the panel adjustments so that the keyboard may be infinitely transposed. On some synthesizers it is possible to *attenuate* the control output of the keyboard in order to reduce the size of the intervals played. This will allow for the performer to play perfectly proportioned microtones.

Most synthesizers have a *portamento control* which, when turned on, allows the control voltage to glide from the keyboard setting previously used to the following one. The result of this is glissando or portamento from one note to the next. A potentiometer is used to determine the amount of glide.

The ARP and some Moog synthesizers have as regular equipment a form of linear voltage control. On the Moogs, it is a hand-operated *ribbon controller* which enables the performer to slide a finger along a band of metallic ribbon. The device puts out a control voltage in direct proportion to the position of the performer's finger on the ribbon. Most manufacturers have as optional equipment a linear controller in the form of a foot pedal. This device (standard with ARP) has the same function as the ribbon controller, but leaves the performer's hands free for other manipulations. Linear controllers provide voltages for sliding and glissandi effects, when connected as control sources to the oscillators.

A relatively simple source of control voltages is a control mixer with a set of switches and potentiometers. This type of device allows the performer to set specific control voltages for each switch and then "play" the switches in some order. This type of control appears on the Electrocomp and Buchla synthesizers. The Electrocomp uses push-button switches similar to those on telephone dials. The Buchla has a more elaborate and more flexible system which uses touch-sensitive plates for switching. The layout of the plates is designed to allow the performer the option of "playing" them like a keyboard or sliding rapidly back and forth to produce unusually rapid changes in the control voltages. Control mixers of that sort could be represented by the following diagram:

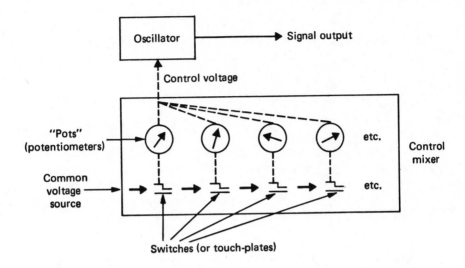

The Synthi AKS incorporates, besides its keyboard controller, a "joystick" device which, rotating on an axis, provides two possible control voltages which may be mixed in any proportion by the performer. These may be used to control any two *parameters* of the instrument, the most obvious being pitch and amplitude.

FREQUENCY MODULATION

One of the most important widely used techniques of electronic music is that of frequency modulation. In its simplest sense, this is the use of one oscillator to change (modulate) the pitch (frequency) of another. Remember that the output of an oscillator is a voltage waveform. This voltage can be applied directly to the control inputs of another oscillator being used to provide the signal. One oscillator therefore becomes the "control oscillator" and the other the "signal oscillator." On most synthesizers, one or more oscillators are prewired to be used as "control oscillators" with the performer switching the output of these oscillators on and off as desired. In some instruments, these modules are designed not to operate in the audio range and only to produce relatively slow frequencies. They are then referred to by the manufacturers as

77

subaudio waveform generators. The following diagram represents the basic flow chart for frequency modulation:

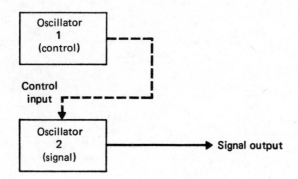

Note how, in the following diagram, the frequency of the signal oscillator is changed in direct proportion to the shape of the controlling waveform:

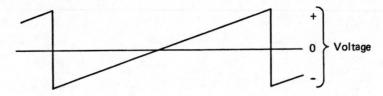

(A) The output of oscillator 1, a slow-frequency sawtooth waveform

(B) The output of oscillator 2 without modulation, a steady-pitch square wave

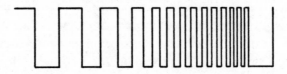

(C) The resultant output of oscillator 2 with modulation. The frequency increases in proportion to the amplitude increase of the controlling waveform.

The resulting "sound" will depend upon several factors. The repetition of each modulation will depend upon the frequency of the control oscillator. Second, the range of the pitch interval covered by the modulation will depend upon the amplitude of the control oscillator. When the control oscillator is set at low frequencies, the *timbre* of the signal remains unchanged. In the above diagram, it is still clearly a square wave. The *vibrato* of an electric organ is usually achieved in this manner. This can be duplicated on a synthesizer by using a slow-frequency (around 3-8 Hz.) sine wave with a very small amount of amplitude to modulate a signal. As the frequency of the control is increased, the vibrato will speed up, and as the amplitude is increased, the vibrato will "widen."

When the frequency of the control oscillator reaches the area of audio (around 30 Hz.), the sound of the frequency modulation will begin to distort the timbre of the original signal. As the modulation frequency is increased, more and more "sideband" frequencies are produced. The results are sounds that are clangorous, bell-like tones, unique—and valuable—to electronic music.

OSCILLATOR MIXERS

All synthesizers are equipped with mixers for combining more than one oscillator. (The Roland SH3 employs only one audio oscillator, but includes a mixer to combine 5 octave settings from this oscillator.) They are also capable of "gang-controlling" more than one oscillator to a single control device. This will, of course, allow the performer the opportunity of "playing" more than one oscillator, setting up chords which can be transposed to every key of the keyboard, combining waveforms on a single note, enriching a tone with artificially added harmonics, and so forth. A flow chart of one possible setup could be represented as follows:

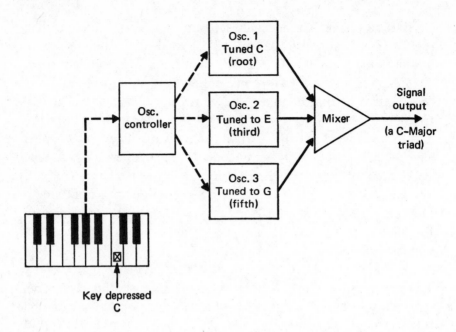

In the above flow chart, the three oscillators are tuned to a triad. This chord will "track" the keyboard. If, for example, the note D is depressed, the chord will become D, F sharp, A. If the key pressed is B flat, the chord will become B flat, D, F. Tunings are arbitrary, of course, and therefore are open to the performer's experimentation.

VOLTAGE-CONTROLLED AMPLIFIERS

The voltage-controlled amplifier and its companion module, the envelope generator, are the *articulators* of the synthesizer. The output of the audio oscillators requires additional amplification before it has enough power to provide a signal to an external monitor. This amplification takes place in a unqiue device controlled by external voltages. On most small synthesizers, the VCA is not shown on the panel. Since it is an important part of the synthesizer, however, we shall examine it and include it in the basic flow chart as follows:

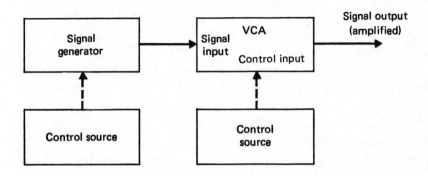

In an ordinary audio amplifier, the amount of amplification is controlled by a potentiometer which is the volume control. In a voltage-controlled amplifier, control voltages are used to increase or decrease the desired amplitude. The VCA has two inputs, one for signal and the other for control. It has one output, which is the final output section of the synthesizer. The usual source of control voltages for the VCA is an *envelope generator,* sometimes called a *contour generator.* This module must be activated by some sort of *trigger.* Whenever it is triggered, it produces one flow of DC voltage directly to the control section of the VCA. This, in turn, amplifies (thereby "turning on") the signal which is entering it.

The envelope generator can be triggered every time a key is depressed on the keyboard. Envelope generators may also be triggered with the outputs of a pulsewave generator or even with manual push buttons. The DC voltage that is produced by the generator at each triggering can be adjusted by the performer in several ways. Although this will vary slightly on different instruments, the concept remains the same. It can best be seen in a diagrammed form.

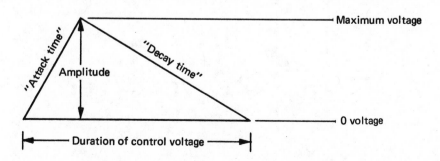

81

The duration of the control voltage will become the duration of the musical tone. The amplitude will become the loudness, and the *attack* and *decay* times will represent the tone's attack and the time it takes to die away. In order to approximate more closely actual instrumental articulations, synthesizers have controls over not only the attack and decay but also the *sustain* amplitude and *release* times. The diagram below refers to all standard envelope controls. (On most instruments, decay and release times are automatically the same; others have controls for release time.)

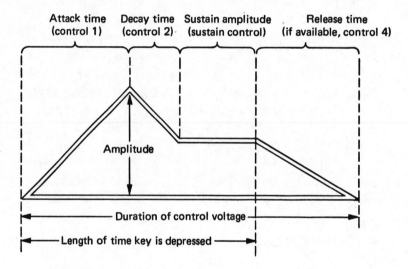

ARP and Roland synthesizers incorporate sliding potentiometers in their envelope generators (which both manufacturers refer to as ADSR modules). These visually relate to the diagram above and look like this:

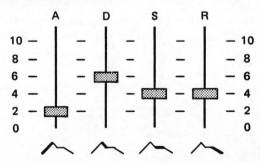

As can be seen now, as a key is depressed on a synthesizer, two switches are generally activated simultaneously. One releases a control voltage to the oscillators while the second provides a trigger to the envelope generator. This enables the keyboard to function as a traditional musical instrument, providing both pitch and articulation.

There are a number of variations available for obtaining triggers. One of the most common is to use the output of a pulsewave generator. This may be any subaudio generator, and in most cases the wiring for this has been manufactured into the instrument. What occurs in this case is that each positive pulse will become a trigger for the envelope generator. This is shown as follows:

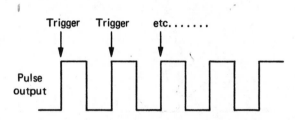

Using a trigger of this sort will enable the performer to play rapid staccato repetitions, drumbeats in specific tempos, drumrolls, and many other effects.

AMPLITUDE MODULATION

The first discussion of voltage-controlled amplifiers noted that these modules are built into most small synthesizers and do not appear on the face panels. In most cases, however, there is either a control input for patching an external source, or a switch for the internal patching of a control oscillator. The purpose of these controls is to obtain from the amplifier the effect known as *amplitude modulation*.

In the same simple sense in which frequency modulation was defined, we may look at amplitude modulation as the use of one oscillator to change (modulate) the loudness (amplitude) of a signal. Since we already understand that the output wave-

83

form of an oscillator can provide a control voltage, it is necessary only to apply that voltage to the control input of the VCA to achieve amplitude modulation.

To demonstrate the effect a particular waveform can have on an amplified signal, note that in the following diagram the amplitude changes in direct proportion to the shape of the controlling waveform:

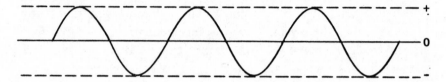

(A) The output of controlling oscillator, a low-frequency sine wave

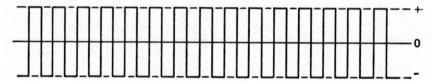

(B) A pulse wave signal, amplified at a steady, sustained level

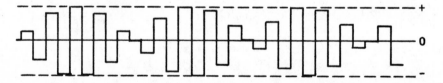

(C) The resultant output of the voltage-controlled amplifier with the amplitude of (B) modulated by waveform (A)

The "sound" of amplitude modulation depends upon the frequency, amplitude, and waveform of the modulating oscillator. Like frequency modulation, at slow, modulating frequencies the timbre of the original tone is not affected. The obvious result of amplitude modulation is the appearance of a regular increase and decrease in loudness. This type of change, when created on traditional acoustical instruments, is called *tremolo*.

84

As with frequency modulation, it is possible to achieve complex timbres through the addition of "sidebands" produced by using as a controlling oscillator one producing audio frequencies. Further unusual tonal possibilities may be obtained by experimenting with different waveforms as modulators.

CONCLUSION

This chapter has presented the first concepts relating to the electronic music synthesizers. The material presented has covered the generation of sounds, pitch control, frequency modulation (vibrato), mixers for the combining of tones, loudness and articulation, and amplitude modulation (tremolo). As a means of reviewing some of these, study the next flow chart. It represents the interval of a perfect fifth (C and G) with a slow vibrato. The sound has a clarinetlike quality (determined by the use of square waves) and has a short plucked attack followed by a moderately short decay.

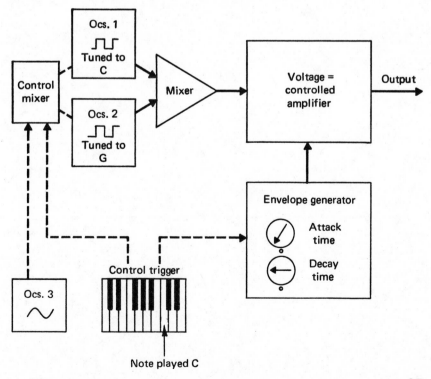

85

TERMINOLOGY FOR STUDY

Before going on to "In the Studio," it is very important that you understand the following terms. Be able to define them in your own words.

control voltage
analog device
signal
audio range
oscillator
keyboard controller
attenuation
linear controller
control mixer
parameter
frequency modulation
subaudio generator

controlling oscillator
voltage-controlled amplifier
envelope generator
timbre
vibrato
tremolo
articulation
trigger
attack and decay
sustain amplitude
release time
amplitude modulation

6

ELECTRONIC MUSIC SYNTHESIZERS (2)

Chapter V discussed the modifications of the output signal from a waveform generator in terms of frequency and amplitude modulations and envelope control. Modifications of the *timbre* of a signal are also necessary in the production of interesting musical events. *Timbral modification* is not only used in synthesizer-generated music, but is essential in the manipulation of music to be produced from tape-recorded sources (*musique concrète*).

A sine wave produces no overtones, but all other waveforms generated by electronic music synthesizers produce a variety of overtones in varying amplitudes. The fundamental tone and the overtones generated from this fundamental are referred to as the *spectrum* of the sound. It is this overtone spectrum that creates the qualities that we recognize as specific timbres. Listen carefully to each waveform available and consider its *harmonic content*. (The harmonic content is the spectrum of the tone and refers to the number of overtones produced and their relative amplitudes.)

1. Sine wave	No overtones produced	Very "pure" tone; flutelike
2. Sawtooth wave	Produces all overtones decreasing in loudness exponentially	"Bright" tone with a double-reed type of sound

3. Square wave	Produces only odd-numbered harmonics, with amplitude decreasing in linear manner	"Woody" character, almost like a clarinet
4. Triangular wave	Produces odd-numbered harmonics sharply falling off in amplitude	Slightly more reedy than a sine, almost like a recorder

The following chart shows the overtones produced by the four principal waveforms as represented by musical notes. In each case, the fundamental tone produced is C two octaves below middle C.

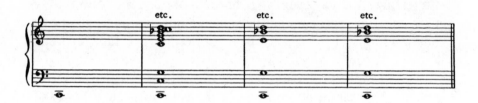

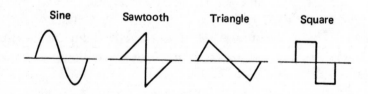

Remember that although the chart above represents the same tones produced by square and triangular waves, the difference in the amplitudes of the overtones creates a totally different timbre between the two.

An almost infinite number of variations of the above waveforms can be produced by most synthesizers. In some cases it is possible to produce two waveforms simultaneously from the same oscillator. Some instruments provide a means of gradually changing from one waveform to another by means of a potentiometer on the faceplate. It is also possible to combine oscillators "in unison" with more than one waveform, or build up synthetic waveforms (if enough oscillators are available) by means of adding sine waves in some nonharmonic ratio. The most common, and simplest, way of modifying or synthesizing timbres is to incorporate a filter into the operational flow chart of sound production. In essence, this would be represented in the following manner:

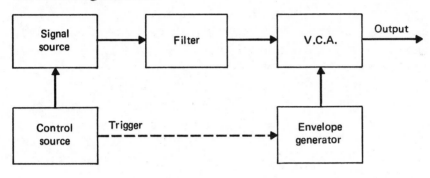

LOW-PASS FILTER

Simply defined, a filter is a device that allows some frequencies to pass, but blocks (or filters out) other undesired frequencies. Since filter packages frequently include amplifiers, these filters can actually make certain sounds louder while diminishing or completely removing others. The most common filter used in synthesizers is the *low-pass filter*. This device will allow all of the sound spectrum to pass *below* a certain adjustable frequency. The point at which the amplitude of the passed spectrum begins to drop is called the *frequency cutoff point*. The next diagram represents a sound passed through a low-pass filter. In this case the frequency cutoff point is at 750 Hz. You will notice that the loudness begins to drop off at this point, but does not fall off at a right angle. Such a filter having ideal filtering functions is not obtainable on any synthesizer.[1]

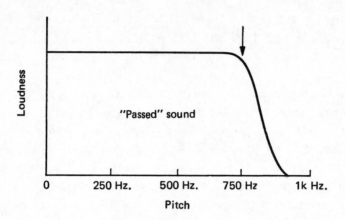

For a further examination of the low-pass filter, study the following diagrams. They represent a complex sound (many harmonics) with a fundamental frequency of 256 Hz. (middle C). The *cutoff* is also set at 256 Hz., and the sound that results from filtering would be a sine-wave tone on the middle C. This sine-wave timbre would be the same no matter what the original spectrum was, since fundamental tones are always sine waves, and the filter has removed all overtones from the original source.

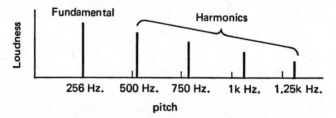

(A) Original "complex" wave (overtones present)

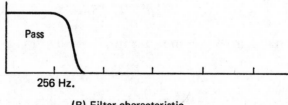

(B) Filter characteristic

90

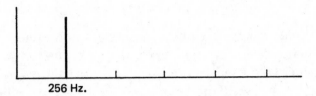

256 Hz.

(C) Only the 256 Hz. can get "through" the filter

With the additional use of voltage control and regeneration, both of which will be discussed later in this chapter, the filter can be used to duplicate the "colors" of many traditional instruments as well as to produce those sounds unique to the electronic medium.

HIGH-PASS FILTER

Not all of the small synthesizers have the high-pass filter. It is very useful in musical applications since its function (the reverse of that of the low-pass filter) allows the performer to "cut out" fundamentals while hearing only the harmonics or upper partials of a tone. The use of a high-pass filter can have a very interesting effect upon the perception of tones, since the intervallic relationships between the overtones becomes closer in higher partials. The effect, once the fundamental has been filtered out, is an eerie, muted dissonance.

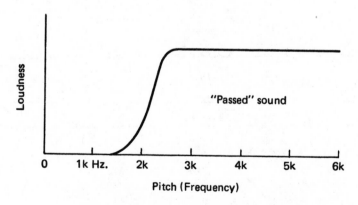

High pass filter with a cut-off of 2500 (2.5k) Hz.

91

BAND-PASS FILTER

The *band-pass filter* eliminates all sound on either side of a narrow center band. In most cases, the *bandwidth* (the interval of frequencies covered by the band) and the *center frequency* (the pitch directly in the center of this band) are adjustable. Although most synthesizers do not have a separate band-pass filter, it is usually possible to control the low-pass filter with a regeneration that achieves band-pass results. (It might be noted that the Electrocomp (EML) and Roland SH5 synthesizers have a multi-function filter that may be adjusted from high to low pass through a band pass.) This regeneration device will be discussed later.

In one sense, it may be helpful to think of a band-pass filter as the product of a low- and high-pass filter wired together in series, with the output of the low going into the input of the high. When the two cutoff frequencies overlap, a band of passed sound will remain in the center. The width of this band may be controlled by either of the two pots controlling cutoff frequency, and the center frequency will be controlled by turning both in the same direction simultaneously. This type of device would be diagramed as shown:

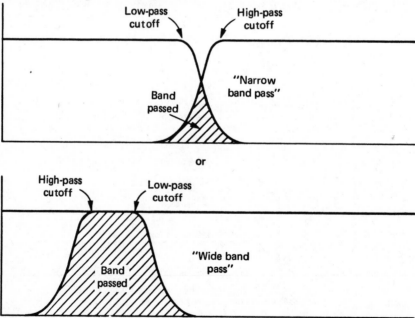

The low-pass removes all sound from the right of the cutoff point, and the high-pass removes all sound from the left. The "pass" that remains is the reuslt of overlapping these points.

BAND-REJECT FILTER

This type of filter does not exist on the smaller synthesizers. Its function is to pass all sound on *either side* of a center band, and so may be thought of as the opposite of the band-pass filter. A *band-reject* filter may be made easily by connecting both a low- and a high-pass filter in parallel. The same signal would then be sent into both filters at the same time, and their outputs would be remixed. The low pass will pass only the low range of pitches while the high pass will pass only the high pitches. The resulting effect can be most interesting, especially when it is applied to sawtooth or square wave tones. (Only the fundamental and the very distant partials will be heard.)

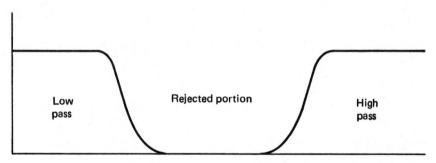

FIXED FILTER BANK

The larger Moog, ARP, and Buchla systems are all equipped with *fixed filter banks.* These consist of a series of filters, each capable of controlling one band of the spectrum. Usually the band is fairly wide, but this varies with each filter. A fixed filter bank may have ten or more filters. Each is equipped with one potentiometer to control the amplitude of the band pass. Usually there is a low-pass filter at the low end and a high-pass at the high end.

Because fixed filters offer so many possibilities for shaping the sound spectrum they are quite useful in electronic music. It is possible that they are excluded from the small synthesizers because they would take up too much space on the faceplates. In any case, they would make valuable optional equipment for any home or school studio.

PROGRAM EQUALIZERS

Program equalizers, although not part of any synthesizer, are valuable additions to the electronic studio. Employed by all recording studios and broadcasting facilities, they provide both attentuation and amplification as desired at different points in the audio spectrum. A signal may be equalized to reduce or increase bass, reduce or increase many areas of mid-range sounds, reduce high-frequency noise or add overtone brilliance. Basically these operate in the same manner as the treble and bass controls on a high-fidelity preamplifier. Program equalizers usually are equipped with potentiometers to control eight or more bands. They are generally sliding controls and are calibrated with *flat response* (marked 0) in the center, with a boost and reduction of up to 16db above and below that point.

When producing the final mixed tape (master recording) of a composition it is advisable to employ equalization. A typical faceplate of an equalizer and the response curve that it would produce are shown below:

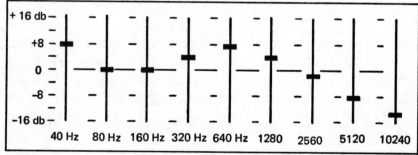

Equalizer (calibrated in octaves)

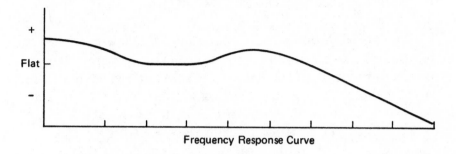

Frequency Response Curve

VOLTAGE-CONTROLLED FILTERS

Use of the *voltage-controlled filter* is extremely important in music. Control voltage can be used to operate any function of these filters, making discrete and rapid timbral change easy to obtain. When working with low-pass filtering, the control voltage will affect the frequency cutoff point. The higher the control voltage, the higher the cutoff point; the lower the control voltage, the lower the cutoff point. As an example, consider an envelope generator that is providing a short attack and long decay to the output of a signal. This same envelope may be applied not only to the voltage-controlled amplifier but also to the voltage-controlled filter. The result will be a tone with a short attack and rich overtone content that decays slowly, while simultaneously losing its harmonics.

As another example of voltage-controlled filtering, it is possible to use the output of an oscillator to control the function of a filter. This will result in imposing the waveform shape of the oscillator's output onto the cutoff frequency of the filter. If a tone rich in harmonics were being played into a voltage-controlled low-pass filter, which was being controlled by a sine wave oscillating at 1 or 2 Hz., the result would be a continual "wah-wah" effect as the frequency cutoff moved back and forth, adding and reducing the overtones.

All synthesizers are designed to provide an envelope which can control the filter. In most cases, two envelope generators are available with one operating the VCA and the other the filter. Control of the filter by an oscillator is also available on every synthesizer, and in most cases external filter control may be employed.

95

REGENERATION

A *regeneration* circuit is built into the low-pass voltage-controlled filters of all synthesizers. Manufacturers use the terms *regeneration, resonance,* or *emphasis* when describing its function. In essence, it creates a "peak" or exaggerated strong tone just before the response drops off at the cutoff point. This exaggeration or *resonance* may be increased in amplitude by a potentiometer. Technically, regeneration isolates a band-pass at the cutoff frequency and feeds this back into the filter's input through the control pot.

The use of regeneration adds considerable emphasis to the functions of a filter, and can be very useful in producing plucked electric bass or guitar sounds. In combination with various control inputs, an endless number of unusual effects can be produced with the regeneration function.

When used with an oscilloscope, the regeneration control offers a unique opportunity to see how waveforms such as the sawtooth are actually complex sine-wave structures. To do this, provide a VC low-pass filter with a sawtooth input. Turn the regeneration up about halfway, and slowly turn the frequency control to add and subtract overtones. The resultant harmonics will be easily heard and seen as additive sine waves on the oscilloscope.

By producing complex waveforms with the regeneration control, it will be possible to synthesize certain sounds approaching vocal quality.

Filters have played a major part in the manipulation of electronic music since the explorative days of *musique concrète.* The available filtering functions of your synthesizer should be explored through continual improvisation until you are able to plan whatever filtering effect you desire.

RANDOM-SIGNAL GENERATORS

All synthesizers have a generator capable of producing output signals which, unlike those produced by an oscillator, are not fixed in frequency and loudness. These generators

96

produce random signals which, on an oscilloscope, appear as follows:

At a low output level, this sounds like radio static or a continuous "shhhhhhh." This signal may be said to contain a random mixture of all frequencies and (by analogy to the frequencies of color) is called *white sound* or *white noise*. The white-noise generator on synthesizers is usually accompanied by a fixed filter which, by boosting amplitude in the lower frequencies, produces a deeper sound called *pink noise*.

The noise generator is generally used in conjunction with a filter. The filtering of a noise signal (which produces what is called banded noise) provides many unusual effects. When applied as an input to a low-pass filter with regeneration, it is possible to obtain the sound of storms and wind by operating the frequency cutoff pot. By incorporating envelope control to both the filter and the voltage-controlled amplifier simultaneously, it is possible to simulate many different percussive sounds by using white or pink noise as a signal. It is also possible to combine noise with signals to produce various effects. The following flow chart represents the use of a noise generator to create the sound of a snare drum:

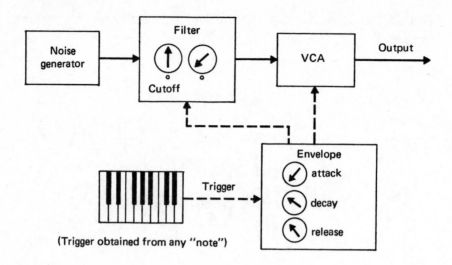

(Trigger obtained from any "note")

The settings given were designed for a MiniMoog synthesizer. Experimentation will achieve the same basic results on any instrument. If the synthesizer has a separate envelope control for the filter, set it the same as the loudness envelope.

REVERBERATION UNITS

All of the large studio synthesizers and some of the smaller models are equipped with *reverberation* units. Originally designed to add "space" and realism to recordings, the reverb unit is more frequently used in electronic music as another device to distort or modify signals. Reverberation extends the duration of a sound event by adding to the initial event a series of "reflections" (very rapid echoes) of that event. True acoustic reverberation takes place in any large hall, where music or other sound seems to "hang in the air" after it has been produced.[2]

Artificial reverberation is produced by a *spring-type reverb*. This device consists of a signal input, signal output, and one potentiometer. In its operation, a signal is applied through a coil, much like that on a speaker, to a metal spring or pair of springs through which it travels as vibrations. These vibrations are picked up at the opposite end of the spring by means of a microphone pickup. The potentiometer is used to control a mixer combining the original signal with the reverberated signal. This gives the performer control over the amount of desired reverb.

When operating a spring reverb, care must be taken not to suddenly jar the instrument, since any excessive movement of the spring will be picked up as distortion.

Although most small synthesizers do not have spring reverb units, it is possible to buy them from the manufacturers who build them for pop music applications. Reverb units called space expanders have also been produced for the home high-fidelity market.

CONCLUSION

The skillful use of filters will provide some of the most valuable manipulations to the composer of electronic music. It is absolutely imperative that the functions of whatever sort of filter is available be mastered. The voltage-controlled low-pass filter function is built into every synthesizer. Some synthesizers have the additional possibilities of band- and high-pass filters. Large studio units have filter couplers to provide voltage-controlled band-pass and band-reject functions. Filter-function diagrams are very helpful visual devices. Study them throughout the chapter and compare the diagrams to the sounds that you achieve.

The noise generator is used to produce many unpitched effects. Used with an envelope, it provides countless percussive sounds and can be banded and shaped through filtering for other valuable effects.

The use of reverberation either during the process of recording a piece of music or at the time of final "mix-down" can be an effective way of adding spatial dimensions to the work. Experimentation will also prove that it offers many modifications to previously recorded events or oscillator tones.

NOTES

1. The sloping curve which is used to represent the attenuation of loudness following the frequency cutoff point is measured in *decibels per octave*. The industry standard for synthesizers is 24 db per octave.

2. See also page 62.

TERMINOLOGY FOR STUDY

Before going on to "In the Studio," it is very important that you understand the following terms. Be able to define them in your own words.

timbral modification	band-reject filter
spectrum	fixed filter bank
harmonic content	program equalizer
low-pass filter	regeneration
frequency cutoff point	emphasis
high-pass filter	resonance
band-pass filter	reverberation
bandwidth	spring reverb
center frequency	

7

ELECTRONIC MUSIC SYNTHESIZERS (3)

The more complex modules designed into electronic music synthesizers will be discussed in this chapter. Until quite recently, they were available only as separate units, to be added as components to an electronic studio. Developments in sub-miniaturization and integrated circuits within the past few years have led to the inclusion of one or more of these functions in all but the MiniMoog. Each can be used to produce complex and sophisticated electronic effects. The concepts of *voltage control of all modules, waveform shapes,* and *overtones* should be reviewed and completely understood before going on to this chapter.

RING MODULATION

As mentioned in Chapter V, amplitude modulation produces a series of sidebands when the oscillator providing control voltages to the VCA is generating a frequency within the audio range. To be precise, this effect produces sidebands which are related to the signal and to the control oscillator in a very definite manner. The sidebands (which, in amplitude modulation, are soft, but audible) occur above and below the frequency of the signal generated and consist of frequencies mathematically related to the signal and the control (called the *program*) as the *sum and difference* of these two frequencies.

As an experiment, use a signal from a sine-wave generator as a sound source and route it into the voltage-controlled amplifier. As a control voltage to the amplifier, use another sine-wave at subaudio frequencies. The result should be the sound of the signal pulsing in loudness in proportion to the shape, loudness, and frequency of the control. This is the traditional sound of amplitude modulation. Now gradually increase the frequency of the control (the modulating oscillator). As its frequency approaches the audio range, you will hear a low frequency and a high frequency in the output. What you hear, besides the original signal, are the sum and difference frequencies of both the original and the control.

For the sake of clarity, assume that a steady signal (or *carrier*) of 200 Hz. is being heard as the original sound. The control (or *program*) begins at 5 Hz. and gradually is increased until it reaches 200 Hz. Sum and difference frequencies will become audible as the program reaches about 30 Hz., as represented by the diagram below. Notice that in amplitude modulation, the control is not heard itself.

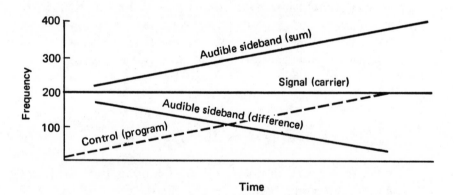

It was suggested that the experiment be done with two sine waves. Any other combinations of waveforms will produce a number of different sidebands and a considerably more complex sound structure. This is because *each of the overtones of the original waveforms will produce its own series of sidebands.* Extremely clangorous sounds will be produced when using waveforms rich in harmonics.

102

Ring modulation is a form of amplitude modulation in which *any* two signals are used as inputs (program and carrier) to the modulator. The output of the device will be only the sum and difference frequencies, while both original signals will be suppressed. On a synthesizer, ring modulation offers many advantages over amplitude modulation. Since amplitude modulation incorporates a voltage-controlled amplifier, one of the two sources, the program, must always be a generated control voltage. In ring modulation, any signal source may be used, including external signals such as guitar, electric piano, tape recorder, and so on. The sound possibilities offered by incorporating sources rich in harmonic content are endless.

SAMPLE-AND-HOLD

Remembering that control voltages may be used for a countless number of synthesizer operations, we shall now examine one of the more sophisticated devices for the production of control voltages, the *sample-and-hold* module. This device consists of a pulse oscillator which is used as a *clock,* or triggering mechanism. Any signal which is fed into it will be *sampled* at each pulse or trigger. The sampling consists of holding the voltage level of the waveform at the time of a pulse until the next pulse is received.

In the next diagram, a sawtooth wave is used as an input. The clock rate is regular, and due to the effect of the sampling, the sawtooth wave is changed to a waveform referred to as a staircase wave.

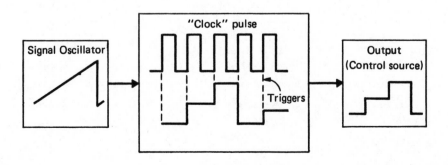

103

The output of a sample-and-hold module is a voltage wave-form that can be used as some sort of control. Since, in the first example shown, the input was a sawtooth wave and the triggering was constant, the output will appear to represent even steps of voltage. If this control voltage were applied to an oscillator, it would produce a series of definitely pitched tones called a *sequence*. If the sampling continued, the sequence would continue to repeat, producing fixed pitches without the use of a keyboard.

Consider a simple variation of the above: the clock trigger remains the same, but instead of a sawtooth wave, the input waveform is the output of a random generator such as pink noise. In this case, an output of control voltages of random amplitude will be achieved. These are often used to create random pitch generation when applied to an oscillator as a control input.

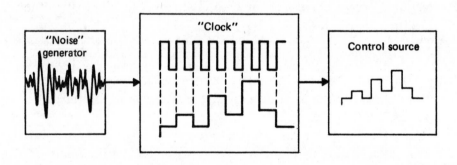

Since there is no recycling of a random event, the voltages produced will remain random continually.

The sampler of the Roland SH3 is a typical example of sample-and-hold modules on a small synthesizer. A four-position switch allows the choice of input waveforms: sawtooth, inverted sawtooth, triangle, and white noise. The switch is marked:

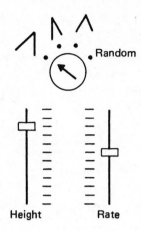

It is, of course, possible to vary the frequency of the pulse generator that provides the trigger. In some cases, this generator is also voltage controlled, allowing for *its* variability, and an extremely wide selection of pulse rhythms may be obtained. It should be remembered that as control voltages, the outputs of the sample and hold can be used to control timbre and rhythm as well as pitch.

ANALOG SEQUENCERS

Sequencers are the most complex and the most interesting modules designed to produce control voltages. They are used for the creation and control of *repeated musical events* (in classical music they would be called ostinati or ground basses). Of the small synthesizers being discussed in this text, only the SYNTHI AKS is equipped with a sequencer, and its digital unit will be discussed further on in this chapter. All synthesizer manufacturers do produce sequencers, however, and they may be purchased to augment any existing system.

An *analog sequencer* consists of a series of manually set potentiometers, each providing an output of DC control voltage. These voltages are connected to the output of the unit, one at a time, with the order determined by a pulse

105

"clock" oscillator. An electronic switch called a flip-flop switch is one that is turned *on* by each pulse and is turned *off* when the next switch is triggered. The *pulse rate,* or sequencing rate, is completely controlled by turning a potentiometer on the pulse generator itself. A simplified sequencer is represented below:

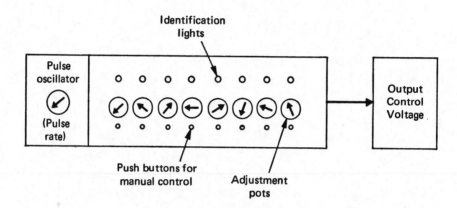

On the sequencer above, there are eight positions. Each has an adjustment to determine the amount of control voltage to be sent to the output, and an identifying light to show when the sequence is at that point. The output of the sequencer may be used to provide voltage control for any oscillator, filter or VCA. It is possible to "tune" a sequencer by hand, setting each position with the pulse oscillator off, and measuring the output voltage. ("Measurement" may be done by ear, using the control to "play" a pitch oscillator.)

Most sequencers have more than one set of adjustment "pots." With these, it is possible to provide simultaneous control voltages to different sections of the synthesizer. In the next flow chart, a sequencer is being used to provide *two* separate control voltages, one to an oscillator, and the other to a voltage-controlled filter. This will allow the performer to repeat any desired pitch and timbral sequences at will.

106

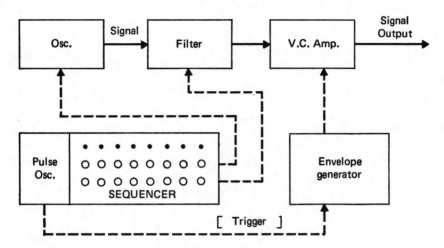

Notice from the above chart that the output of the pulse clock can be used also as a *trigger* for the *envelope generator,* thereby synchronizing each pitch with its own attack and decay characteristics.

An additional function of an analog sequencer is its ability to generate a varying rhythmic pattern. The clock oscillator is a voltage-controlled device. If the output of one adjustment "bank" is used as the control input to the clock, the result will be that larger voltages will delay the firing rate and smaller voltages will speed the firing rate. It is therefore perfectly possible for the following flow chart to produce the accompanying musical event in sequence.

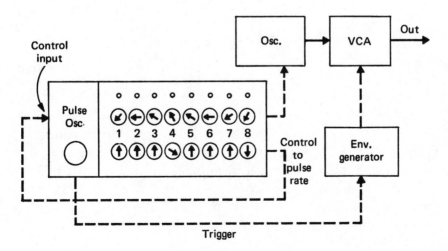

107

If the same setup as above had an additional connection from the output of row 2 to the control input of the voltage-controlled amplifier, it would be possible to include *dynamic changes* in the final output which would relate to the duration of the notes played.

It is possible to interconnect more than one sequencer in order to produce highly complex sequenced patterns. This sort of composition requires a complete control of the entire studio and cannot be considered in the realm of elementary electronic music. Familiarity with the sequencer's functions and usefulness seems to be the threshold for the student moving into advanced techniques. If it is feasible, a sequencer should be incorporated into the studio as soon as a reasonable amount of work is being done.

DIGITAL SEQUENCERS

Analog, as you will remember from Chapter V, refers to a device which employs as some control a measurable voltage "analogous" to the final output of the system. Such a system is the analog sequencer previously discussed. That sequencer uses a power supply to make available control voltages to be used in such operations as tuning oscillators and shifting filters.

Any electronic device correctly referred to as *digital* implies more sophisticated and usually more accurate forms of control incorporating some degree of computer technology. (This use

108

of the term *digital* should not be confused with the word as used by the advertisers of alarm clocks that display time using numbers rather than hands. These may or may not employ digital circuits.) It refers to the technique of storage and processing of information by *binary coding*. Binary coding is a number system using only two values: zero and one. Our familiar decimal system uses ten digit values from zero to nine. The reason that binary coding is used in computer systems is that the two values are represented very nicely by the two fundamental states of a circuit, off and on.

High accuracy is achieved by using many of these on-off circuits at once. For example, ten such circuits will provide an accuracy that will differentiate between the values of 999 and 1,000. "Printed circuits" and "integrated circuits" have made these multiple-circuit systems both cheap and reliable.

At the time of this writing, the only small synthizers with digital circuitry are the SYNTHI and Oberheim. These instruments use a small digital "computer" to transfer the act of touching a key on the keyboard to operating the oscillators of the instrument itself. On the SYNTHI, the same digital system is employed in a built-in sequencer capable of memorizing up to 256 different pitched events with automatic repetition, transposition, speed change, and intervallic variation.

In normal performance, a *short-term memory* stores a "word" consisting of six "bits" of binary information. Each of these "bits" consists of either a *zero* or a *one*. Each will therefore instruct a certain circuit to be either *off* or *on*. The first five bits locate the note that was played. The sixth bit is an instruction for triggering or nontriggering. The note location works in the following manner: The first bit divides the keyboard in half (the left half for a 1, the right half for a 0). The second bit divides that half in half, the third bit divides that half, and so on. The fifth bit determines which of the final two half steps was played. This complete unit, or "word," is stored until the next key is depressed. The short-term memory storage is connected to a digital-to-analog converter. This device supplies the analog voltage necessary to operate the control function of an oscillator. It also provides the trigger that operates the envelope generator.

109

The flow chart for this function is represented below:

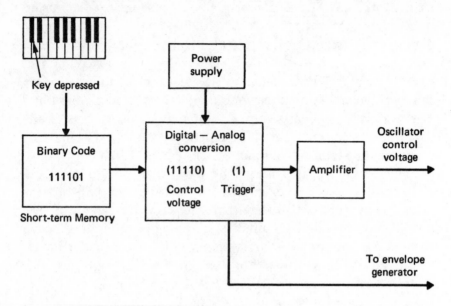

Although more precise control-voltage measurements are made possible with digital circuitry, the most important reason for this type of operation is the ease with which digital information in the form of "words" can be sequenced. Referring once more to the SYNTHI, when the synthesizer is set to "record" a sequence, the storage of each word in the short-term memory is fed through a "clock" into a long-term memory unit with 256 storage places. As the clock clicks forward, anything that is stored in short-term memory will be placed automatically in one or more storage locations of the long-term memory.

For example, if a key is depressed for six seconds, and the clock is clicking away at a rate of two clicks per second, a total of 12 places will be used up in the long-term storage. The first place will store the "word," with the last bit a 1 representing a trigger. The remaining 11 places will also store the control voltage information with a 0 as the last bit. This will not carry a triggering command, and will result in the sustainment of the given pitch.

110

The clock rate is adjustable, and can move to all 256 points within two seconds. It can also be slowed down to take up to four minutes per sweep. When all 256 points are used up, the clock begins again at point one. There are two modes of operation on this type of digital sequencer—record, or play. The record mode is actually a storage mode. During this time, anything played on the keyboard (short-term memory) will be stored in the long-term memory. If, during this mode, the clock reaches all 256 places, it will start over again, erasing anything previously placed in the memory and replacing it with new information.

The play mode disconnects the short-term memory. During this mode, anything stored in the long-term memory will automatically be fed to the digital-analog converter and used to control the synthesizer itself. It is possible to store up to 256 notes and play them back in a repeated sequence with this device. Furthermore, the playback speed can be altered at will, and the sequence will be "remembered" as long as the record mode is not again used.

Digital keyboard circuitry has the added advantage of making instantaneous transpostions and intervallic modifications available. With the sequencer, these effects are most unusual, and are unique to the digital synthesizer.

The digital sequencer discussed in this chapter has been that of the SYNTHI synthesizer. Other digital sequencers available are made to be compatible in control voltage with any of the popular synthesizers. Integrated circuits and subminiaturization of many electronic components make this type of control unit very attractive in the area of musical application. Within a short time, I would venture the guess, at least one more of the major synthesizer makers will be offering complete digital operation in a small synthesizer. This type of technology should produce an instrument capable of true polyphonic operation as well as the recording of extensive sequences in its memory circuits. Not only will the stored sequences be used as in the present SYNTHI, but they will be capable of being stopped at any given point, reversed at will, and stored in their entirety for future use while the synthesizer continues its normal operation.

111

Simplified Flow Chart of a Digital Sequencer in the "Play" Mode.

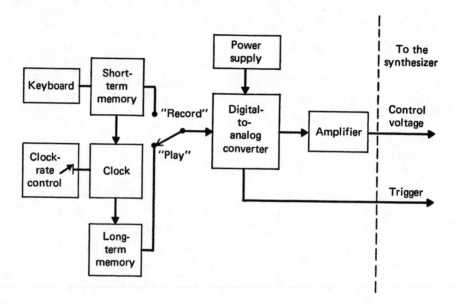

SUMMARY

The ring modulator is generally used to alter sound and to produce clangorous and discordant tones. It may also be used as a source of control voltages in certain setups. The sample-and-hold and sequencers are used mainly for the production of control voltages. These voltages are available for the control of pitch, rhythm, timbre, or their combinations.

Analog sequencers are manufactured by Moog, Buchla, ARP, Roland, and Electrocomp (EML), but are not available on the smaller instruments discussed in this book. In all cases, they can be added as later options in more sophisticated studios.

Digital sequencers are manufactured by SYNTHI, with the SYNTHI AKS and DKS incorporating them as standard equipment. Larger units are made by this corporation and may be used with other synthesizers. There are also a few independent manufacturers who make digital sequencers for use in electronic music.

112

The musical effects obtained through the use of ring modulation and sequencing (either with sample-and-hold generators or actual sequencers) are unique to electronics and should be studied carefully and used with utmost discretion. One of the most serious problems in electronic music is the overuse of sounds that can be obtained only by the medium itself. Listeners are quick to identify those sounds and to tire of their exaggerated or unnecessary use.

There is an old adage used in the world of musical performance which goes, "When in doubt, trill!" After listening to the many synthesized radio and television commercials and pop albums of "switched-on" electronic music released since 1968, one might change that to "When in doubt, sequence!" (A sequel to this would be "When in further doubt, echo! and when all else is lost, put echo on the sequence!")

TERMINOLOGY FOR STUDY

Before going on to "In the Studio," it is very important that you understand the following terms. Be able to define them in your own words.

sum-and-difference frequencies
ring modulator
carrier
program
clock
sample-and-hold
sequence
sequencer
electronic switch
binary coding
word
bit
storage

RECORDED EXAMPLES

SIDE ONE

Band 1   Tape Study # 1   Examples of speed change

Band 2   Tape Study # 1   Tape reversal

Band 3   Tape Study # 2   Composite sounds

Band 4   Tape Study # 3   Tape loop

Band 5   Tape Study # 4   Examples of sound-on-sound using the above techniques.

SIDE TWO

Band 6   Tape Study # 6   Sampling of Musique Concrète. Excerpt from "A Branch of My Anguish" (H. A. Deutsch)

Band 7   Tape Study # 6   Sampling of Musique Concrète. Excerpt from "Circe" (H. A. Deutsch)

Band 8   Synthesizer Study # 1   "Now Thank We All Our God" (1st version)

Band 9   Synthesizer Study # 2   "Now Thank We All Our God" (2nd version)

Band 10   Synthesizer Study # 3   "Electrophunk in A" (H. A. Deutsch)

114

APPENDIX

IN THE STUDIO

The purpose of this appendix is to present, in easy-to-follow form, a series of practical studies designed to supplement Chapters III, V and VI. These studies represent introductory technical and compositional material which has proven effective as a practical teaching aid.

The recording included with the book provides examples of most of these exercises. Although it should be a valuable guide, it doesn't represent the only way of realizing the studies. The number of variables, especially in *musique concrète,* is almost infinite. The recording should represent only a starting point for your own imagination and creativity.

CHAPTER III – THE TAPE RECORDER AS A MUSICAL INSTRUMENT

**Study 1   Experiments in Tape Speed
and Direction**

a.   Set up the tape recorder and microphone in the normal manner. Record your own voice at low speed. Play back at high speed. Reverse the procedure, recording at high speed and playing back at low speed.

b. Tape reversal can be accomplished only on a stereo or *full track monaural* recorder. Record your voice on one track. (With a stereo recorder, use track A.) Pick up the reels, turn over the tape, and reverse the reels onto the opposite hubs of the machine. If you have recorded on a stereo machine, the sound will now appear in reverse on track B. (Note: you must turn track B to *playback.*)

c. After experimenting with your voice (using tongue clicks, whistling, whispers and other vocal sounds), it is desirable to employ the same manipulations with previously recorded sounds. Using a cassette recorder, go outside to record engines, machines, birds, trains, and other sounds. (Sound-effects recordings are readily available and can be most interesting for sound sources.) Experiment with these sounds by using the effects of speed change and tape reversal. You must, of course, transfer the recordings from the cassette to the reel-to-reel recorder for this purpose.

Study 2 Creating Composite Sounds

a. A simple composite sound may be made by combining the *attack* of one sound with the *decay* of a second sound. In order to do this, the sounds must be first located on the tape and then spliced together.

b. *Procedures:* To locate the sound, move the tape by hand with the recorder on, and on *playback,* but with the motors not running. The tape must be moving firmly against the heads. When a sound is heard, it will be located at the *playback,* or third, head. Moving the tape slowly from left to right, mark the point on the tape at the playback head when the sound first occurs. Use a grease pencil or soft marking pen. This is the point of *attack.* (The mark should be made on the tape directly over the center of the head. Do *not* mark the head itself when doing this or any other editing procedure.) Splicing should be done on an open splicing block. For details see diagram in Chapter III.

c. Complex composite sounds can be very effective devices in a musical composition. Select the sounds carefully. You may wish to use certain sounds after slowing, speeding, or reversing them previously.

116

Study 3 Tape Loops

a. Tape loops are used to produce *ostinato* or continually sustained effects. To prepare an ostinato loop, record a continuous nonchanging sound such as a motor or a sustained musical tone with no change in loudness. Determine the length of the loop and prepare it according to the diagrams in Chapter III.

b. When using tape loops, two tape recorders are needed. One will be used to play the loops and the second to record them as needed for the final composition.

c. As in study 2, the recorded sounds to be used in a tape loop should be carefully selected and modified as desired by speed or directional change in order to satisfy any compositional needs. If the loop is made from one sustained sound, and an ostinato is desired, be sure to *splice off* the initial attack before making the loop. Carefully determine that the loudness levels at the beginning and ends of the loop are the same. If a loop is to be made using composite sounds, it should be produced as shown in the following diagram:

(A)

(Selected sounds)

Order of events on tape:

5	4	3	2	1

NOTE: in the above diagram, the oxide side is facing down.

(B) Events spliced into a loop:

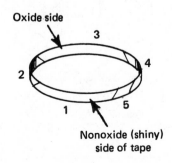

Oxide side

Nonoxide (shiny) side of tape

Study 4 Sound-on-Sound

a. Since the process for using sound-on-sound varies somewhat with each tape recorder, it is advisable that you study the manufacturer's instructional manual thoroughly before you begin any exercises in sound-on-sound techniques. A detailed explanation of the basic principles of sound-on-sound can be found in Chapter III.

b. It is advisable that a number of experiments with sound-on-sound be done. First, using only a microphone and vocal sounds, record a simple background of rhythmic pulses. Set the recorder for sound-on-sound, and, while listening to the previous recording, add additional vocal sounds. By resetting the sound-on-sound, it will be possible to hear both recorded sounds while adding a third. Continue the procedure for a fourth set of sounds.

c. The above procedure may also be used to add harmonic or contrapuntal effects when only one traditional instrument can be played at one time.

d. When recording for a sound-on-sound tape, always set the recording levels to record the highest possible signal without distortion. Each preceding voice can be mixed at the desired level, but the recording levels should be high to increase the signal-to-noise ratio as explained in Chapter III.

Study 5 Tape Echo

a. Any commercially available tape recorder that produces sound-on-sound is also capable of echo effects. It is not possible to produce echo beyond the first recording if you are planning to do a sound-on-sound tape, however, unless an external mixer is used (see Chapter III).

b. To produce echo using only the tape recorder, it is again advisable to consult the manufacturer's instructions. If the recording channel of the machine can be monitored during recording, it will be possible to use an external mixer to combine the monitored signal with the input signal to produce the echo. If this feature is not available, echo will be produced using the tape recorder's sound-on-sound circuit.

c. Reminder: the variables of tape echo are the *loudness* of the echo and the *number of echoes* heard as well as the *time between* each echo. Tape speed and the distance between the record and playback heads determine the time between echoes, the playback level determines the number of echoes heard, and the recording level determines the overall loudness.

Study 6 A Composition of Musique Concrète

After completing the first five studies, the student may venture into a complete work, using the tape recorder as the primary instrument and employing some or all of the techniques already discussed. No step-by-step directions can be given for this study, since creativity and the concept of the work being created will be up to the individual. The recording includes two examples of music composed with only microphone and tape recorder. They are provided only as samples of what can be done relatively easily.

The first sample is from a dance score and was composed more than two years before the Moog synthesizer was developed. The composition was done with a two-track stereo SONY tape deck, the manufacturer's standard microphones, a piano, a suspended cymbal, and some rhythm band instruments similar to those found in all kindergartens. The effect desired in this section was to portray a dream, a nightmare of tormented yearning.

The second example was recorded entirely in a junior high school and is made up of sounds of the school, most of which have been changed, by speed or directional alteration, and made into tape loops. The loops were played by two tape recorders and recorded onto a third. An interesting composite sound may be heard, followed by a recording of the wind at the very end of the sequence.

Musique Concrète presents a considerable challenge to the beginning composer. Its almost limitless vocabulary of possible sounds demands the utmost care in organization and selection. The rewards are many, however, as the results can be eerie, mysterious, hilarious, absurd, or highly communicative. Most important, experiments in musique concrète will develop your knowledge of recording controls and skills. It's fun! Good luck.

CHAPTERS V AND VI
ELECTRONIC MUSIC SYNTHESIZERS (1 AND 2)

Study 1 Bach Chorale "Now Thank We All Our God" (first version)

Having already explored the procedure of sound-on-sound recording through the medium of *musique concrète,* it is now possible to employ multi-tracking along with the synthesizer as the sound source. The well-known Bach chorale no. 330, "Now Thank We All Our God," will be used as an introduction to the concept of applying these recording techniques to a relatively simple four-voice composition. In this version of the chorale, as well as in the second version to be done after this is completed, the recording was made with a MiniMoog synthesizer and a home stereo tape recorder. Instructions will thus refer to this type of equipment. The effects can be produced on any two-oscillator synthesizer and can be approximated even on the smallest one-oscillator unit.

Procedure

a. Set up the synthesizer with the output patched into the left input of the tape recorder. It is helpful to use an external amplifier, if one is available, to monitor the synthesizer, as shown in the following diagram:

120

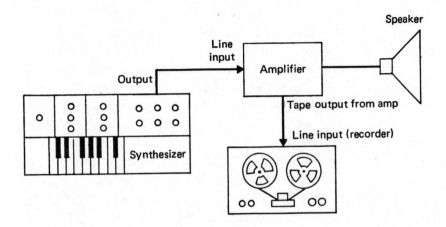

b. It is usually advisable to begin with the bass voice, since it outlines not only the harmonic movement but the rhythmic pulse as well. Always play the line many times to establish a desired tempo and to familiarize yourself with the notes and rhythm. After the tempo has been determined, set a metronome to that speed and practice playing a few times with it. When the recording is made, begin by establishing the beat on the tape. This is done by playing the first note of the piece in the following manner:

In $\frac{3}{4}$ time, play two beats, leaving the third silent.

In $\frac{4}{4}$ time, play three beats, leaving the fourth silent.

When a pickup is present, as in the Bach example, always leave a silent beat before the actual composition is to start. The purpose of this silence is to leave room for splicing off the established beat after the entire recording process has been completed.

On the recording of the first version of the chorale, the two-beat tempo setting has been left on the tape in order to indicate the procedure. Normally it would be removed by splicing prior to the final recording.

c. Voicings: bass — Set two oscillators of the synthesizer to *sawtooth waveforms,* setting them one octave apart with the lower oscillator mixed slightly louder than the upper-tone

121

oscillator. If the synthesizer is calibrated with organ stops (in feet), the lower should be set at 32′ and the upper at 16′. Tune the lower oscillator to play G two octaves below middle C. After the two oscillators are perfectly tuned, adjust one of them slightly *out* of tune in order to produce a very slow "beating" effect, but not enough to produce harsh dissonance. This effect can enhance the timbre of the tone because of the slight phase change taking place.

The envelope should be adjusted to a short attack time (about $\frac{1}{10}$ second), a decay time of about half a second, a sustain time of slightly more than half the maximum amplitude, and a release time of about a half second. The filter will not be used in this version and will remain fully open (no cutoff) with the regeneration down all the way. A very slow vibrato effect may be added by employing frequency modulation from the low-frequency oscillator with a small amount of amplitude.

Examples of the envelope

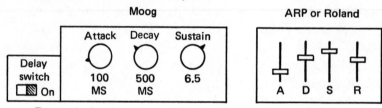

Record the bass line below. Note the tempo notes prior to the actual chorale.

d. Voicings: tenor — The tenor voice is quite similar in color to the bass. Turn off the low oscillator completely and use only the 16′ sawtooth wave. Reduce the amplitude of the vibrato (FM). Set the recorder to the proper sound-on-sound settings so that both voices can be heard while recording. Employing the same envelope control, play the following tenor voice.

122

e. Voicings: alto — The alto voice uses two sawtooth oscillators set in octaves at 8′ and 4′ ranges. They are tuned together with no "chorus" effect (the beating of the slight phase differences used in creating the bass voice). The lower oscillator should be mixed at least twice as loud as the upper oscillator. A buzzy effect is added by employing frequency modulation at a low amplitude but a fairly high rate (approximately 50 Hz.). A very short attack time, half-second decay, half amplitude sustained, and half-second release should be used for envelope. Again, there is no filtering employed.

Record the alto voice from the complete score printed below, making the appropriate recording adjustments to continue the sound-on-sound procedure.

123

   f. Voicings: soprano — For the soprano voice, the two
audio oscillators remain tuned to the 8' and 4' ranges. The mix
is adjusted so that the low pitch is slightly more than half the
loudness of the upper pitch. The lower (8') should remain a
sawtooth waveform while the upper (4') should be switched to
a square wave. Add a low-amplitude vibrato at approximately
6-8 Hz. The envelope of the soprano voice is set for a relatively
long attack time (about .4 second) with a long decay (6-8
seconds) and approximately half-amplitude sustain level. The
release time, like that of the decay, should be quite long.

124

Study 2 "Now Thank We All
Our God" (second version)

The second version of this chorale is presented as an example of the effects of filtering. The voicings chosen for each line of the piece are the same as in the first version, with the exception that each voice is passed through the low-pass voltage-controlled filter and modified by timbral change. An additional portamento (glide) and some tape-head echo are also employed in the soprano voice, as will be explained. Chapter VI should be read and understood before attempting this example.

Procedure

In each case the voices will be set up as before, with the following additions:

a. Voicings: bass and tenor − In order to emphasize the bass quality, a low cutoff frequency should be employed (approximately ¼ of the full open amount). The regeneration (emphasis) should be raised about ⅓, and voltage sensitivity from the envelope generator should be at about ¾ of full.

Examples of the settings

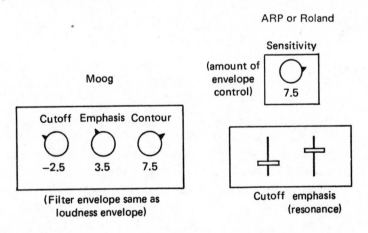

b. Voicings: alto − In order to reduce some of the harshness of the alto voice, a considerable amount of low-pass filtering is employed. Set the cutoff at about ½ of open, add approximately ½ of the full amount of emphasis and ¾ sensi-

125

tivity in order to create a sweeping effect as the decay of the envelope generator activates the filter.

c. Voicings: soprano — If carefully filtered, this soprano can indeed sound quite like that of a human singer. Reduce the cutoff frequency to only about ¼ of open and add about ½ full emphasis. Notice the rather long attack time that had been used on this voice in the first version. If your synthesizer has a separate envelope to generate filter control, set it with the same long attack. Use only about ⅓ of full sensitivity.

A final additional effect will make this an especially interesting voicing. Add portamento (glide) at around ½ of full. Experiment until the tones sweep into pitch with the sound of an actual singer. On the recording of this voice, you may notice a slight echo effect. This can be accomplished with an outside mixer by following the procedure given in Chapter IV. It is not possible to echo the final voice of a sound-on-sound recording unless using an external mixer without adding echo to the total piece.

Study 3 "Electrophunk in A"*

Here is a jazz-rock composition in five voices. On the recording, Roland SH3 and SH1000 synthesizers were used to generate all of the sounds. The recordings were made sound-on-sound, except for the final (melody) voice, which was recorded onto track A of a second tape recorder. An external mixer was used to obtain a slight head echo while the remaining voices were simultaneously recorded onto track B. Both recorders used were ReVox home-type tape machines.

Although this piece might be somewhat difficult for the beginning student of electronic music, realizing it should be a rewarding and valuable experience. A fair amount of keyboard experience is required if this is to be played up to tempo, and it is suggested that a considerably slower speed be used unless the performer feels competent. When recording the final voice, particular care will have to be given to the filter cutoff

*Copyright 1976 by Herbert A. Deutsch.

126

frequency control, which has to be operated with one hand (to create the "wah-wah") while the keyboard is played with the other hand.

a. Voicings: drums — The white-noise or pink-noise generators are used to create this type of drum sound. It will be found that white noise produces better snare or cymbal sounds. If a separate control is built into the synthesizer to allow the keyboard voltage to control the filter (as on the MiniMoog), turn this on. Play the noise generator through the filter, adjusting the cutoff frequency and the emphasis so that the low notes of the keyboard will produce lower-pitched percussive sounds and the upper notes will produce higher-pitched snare drum sounds. The envelope should be set with the shortest attack time, a decay and release time of no more than half a second, and no sustain. The quality of this voice will vary from one synthesizer to another, and some experimentation will be required.

Since this is to be the first voice recorded, and from it all of the rhythmic structure will be derived, considerable attention must be given to the speed of performance and to the establishment of the beat. As with the Bach example, practice the drum part with a metronome, and when recording establish the tempo with three beats, leave a silent fourth beat (for editing), and begin the piece.

The drum part of "Electrophunk" is shown below. Low pitches are played low on the keyboard and high pitches are played high. (Do *not* change the notes that you are using after determining them, since that will change the pitches.)

b. Voicings: bass — An electric bass voice may be produced in a number of ways. This one uses two sawtooth waves tuned in octaves at 32' and 16'. Tune the synthesizer to concert key before beginning. The higher pitch (16') should play the A an eleventh below middle C. Set up the voltage-controlled filter with a low cutoff frequency (approximately ¼ full) and an emphasis of about ⅓ full. Sensitivity to the envelope generator should be at least ½ full. If working with a MiniMoog, turn on both keyboard control voltage switches.

The envelope should employ an attack time of 5 or 10 microseconds, a decay of about half a second and about a one-second release time. No sustain is needed. The setting on a slide-pot envelope generator would look like the following diagram:

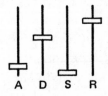

Using sound-on-sound, record the bass line with the drums. Be careful of levels; an electric bass should be recorded quite strong in today's "pop" music. It should never be covered up by the drums. Follow the complete score given in the text when making the recording. Individual parts are not needed.

c. Voicings: upper harmony part – The next voice to add is the upper harmony part. This begins with two sawtooth waveforms also tuned in octaves and at a range of 8' and 4'. These are modulated by a square wave at a rather fast frequency (about 50 Hz.) in order to produce a slightly clangorous quality. In setting up the modulation, do not use an excessive amount of amplitude from the modulating oscillator. About ¼ or less should be employed; more than that will produce too unclear a pitch.

Filter the tone with about ¼ cutoff frequency and ½ full emphasis. Control the filter with about ¾ full sensitivity to the envelope generator. The envelope should have a short attack time (¹/₁₀ second), a decay of at least half a second, and a fair amount of sustain prior to a release time of a half second.

d. Voicings: lower harmony part – This part is voiced similarly to the upper harmony part except that in order to provide a slightly different color and avoid a problem with the phasing of the vibrato effect, all frequency modulation should be removed. Add a bit more regeneration (emphasis) in order to produce a greater fall-off effect and finally lower the output volume of this sound so that in the recording the upper harmony is more pronounced.

e. Voicings: melody – The melody requires three oscillators tuned in octaves (or one oscillator divided into octaves, as with the Roland on which it was made). The low octave (16') should be a square wave, the middle (8') is a sawtooth, and the upper (4') is a sawtooth. They should be mixed so that the 8' voice is the loudest, with the 16' slightly lower and the 4' at only ¼ the loudness of the 8'. No frequency modulation is used in this voice.

The envelope used with the melody is set with a fast attack time and full sustain and decay, with the release time set at ½ full. When the glide effect is used, the setting should be at ¾ full glide amount.

129

The filter and its control are critical in this voice since the filtering will be changed during the performance of the piece. Set the sensitivity *off* so that full control can be made by adjusting the cutoff frequency. The emphasis should be set at about ¾ and adjusted so that a strong "wah-wah" sound is obtained by moving the cutoff frequency control from low to high. The best effects of this device can be achieved only through improvisation and practice, so some time should be spent in playing this voice against the tape without recording it.

If possible, it is advisable not to go beyond four sound-on-sound recording tracks. Therefore a second tape recorder would be helpful in this example since the melody is the fifth voice. Play all four background tracks from the first recorder onto track B of the second recorder, and play the melody onto track A at the same time. It is possible to add echo if an external mixer is used. The block diagram for this setup is shown below:

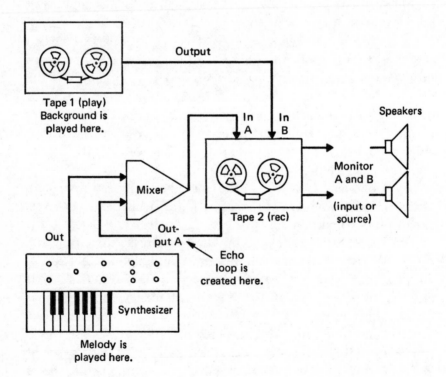

Tape 1 (play)
Background is played here.

Output

In A   In B

Mixer

Tape 2 (rec)

Speakers

Monitor A and B

(input or source)

Out

Out-put A

Echo loop is created here.

Synthesizer

Melody is played here.

131

SYNTHESIS

Repeat entire piece once,
then repeat first 4 bars until fading

132

GLOSSARY OF TERMS

FREQUENTLY USED IN ELECTRONIC MUSIC

acetate The plastic backing used in older recording tapes and found only in the 1½ mil thickness. Desirable for mastering since it would not stretch and cause unwanted distortion.

acoustics A study of the generation, transmission, and perception of sound. Psychoacoustics deals with the effects of sounds on humans. Electroacoustics deals with the electrical generation of sound.

aleatory The determination of musical events by some chance method, such as the use of dice.

amplifier A device used to increase the power or voltage of any signal.

amplitude Usually equated with loudness. The maximum value of a power or voltage during a single cycle of a wave.

amplitude modulation The process of periodically varying loudness. It usually refers to the alteration of a signal's amplitude in order to achieve a tremolo effect. The speed and amplitude alternations are controllable by an external oscillator.

analog device An electronic component in which an output function is directly analogous to some control voltage or voltage waveform.

attack That portion of a tone that occurs following the initiation of the sound and prior to its achieving maximum loudness (*see* envelope).

audio generator An electronic device that produces waveforms within the frequency range of 30 to 20,000 Hertz. Usually referred to as an audio oscillator.

band-pass filter (*see* filter)

band-reject filter (*see* filter)

capstan That portion of a tape recorder consisting of a metal shaft attached to the main motor. The capstan shaft and rubber capstan roller pull the tape past the head assembly at an accurate and desired speed.

clock A device, such as a pulse oscillator, used to operate a sequencer, control sampling, or time the storage of digital information.

control voltage (*see* analog device and voltage control).

decay That portion of a tone after maximum loudness has been reached, and before the end of the tone (*see* envelope).

decibel The standard unit for measuring the loudness of sound. Audible sounds range from approximately 10 decibels (a whisper at about 10 feet) to 120 decibels (the threshold of pain). Abbreviation: db.

digital Refers to any device handling information that can be coded as binary numbers. If the output of such a device is in the form of coded binary numbers, it is referred to as digital output. If the output of such a device is translated into representative voltages, it is referred to as an analog output.

drift The gradual and unintentional shifting of an oscillator away from a fixed value or setting. This may be due to temperature fluctuation or to instrument shortcomings.

dodecaphonic Pertaining to the twelve-tone system of composition.

echo The discernible repetitions of a sound accompanied by gradual decreasing of amplitude (*see* also reverberation and head echo).

envelope The amplitude characteristics that determine the "shape" of a sound in terms of its audible duration. Variables of an envelope are its *attack* (the time taken to reach maximum loudness) and *decay* (the time taken from that point to the end of the signal). Most envelope generators also control *sustain* time, or duration.

equalizer A device that increases or attentuates the strength of a signal in selected portions of the audible spectrum; usually the device used in the mastering process of recording.

erase head The first head of a tape recorder. It erases all previous material on the tape prior to further recording. The erase head is not in operation during the playback mode.

event A single musical entity that is conceived of with all of its dimensions—pitch, duration, loudness, timbre, and so on.

feedback The name given to the reaction when the output or a portion of the output of an amplifier is placed back into the input. Microphone feedback can occur when a microphone used to pick up a sound also picks up the amplification of that sound. In electronic

134

music, the most common form of feedback occurs when a portion of a recording is sent back to the recording amplifier from the playback head (*see* head echo).

filter A device that allows for the selective passing or attentuation of the frequencies of an input signal. There are four basic filter configurations. *High-pass filters* pass all frequencies above a given cutoff point. *Low-pass filters* pass all frequencies below a given cutoff point. *Band-pass filters* pass frequencies only between a high and a low cutoff point. *Band-reject filters* pass all frequencies except those between a high and a low cutoff point.

frequency Vibrations per second of a sound or cycles per second of a waveform. Frequency of a signal in the audible range determines pitch.

frequency modulation The process of periodically varying frequency (*see* amplitude modulation).

gain Increase in amplitude.

harmonics The frequency components present in complex sounds; also called *overtones.* The frequency of a harmonic is an integral multiple of the lowest frequency of the sound (called the *fundamental*).

head configuration The placement of heads in a tape recorder. On professional tape recorders, there are three heads. In the order of tape direction, they are *erase, record,* and *play.*

head echo The specific type of echo effect created when the playback of a signal is rerecorded and played back again. This process is repeated with a gradual decrease in amplitude (*see* feedback).

Hertz After the German scientist Heinrich Hertz, who first detected and measured electrical (electromagnetic) waves; the international name for "cycles per second," abbreviated: Hz.

input The signal which is fed into any device; also the name given to that jack into which the signal is fed.

Klangfarbenmelodie A concept of melody developed by the second Viennese school of the 1920s. Each note (or event) is characterized by its own particular timbre.

mixer A device that makes a composite signal or waveform out of two or more input signals or waveforms.

music Sounds *organized* in time.

monitor A device used to make signals audible during a recording or synthesizing process; an amplifier and speaker or earphones.

modulation The process of varying the waveform of one signal with the output of another signal. Amplitude and frequency are commonly

135

modulated in electronic music. Voltage-controlled filters provide the potential for timbral modulation.

oscillator Strictly speaking, a device that produces alternating current in the form of sine waves. In electronic music, it has become common practice to call any audio generator an oscillator.

oscilloscope An instrument employing a cathode-ray tube which displays graphically the voltage and time characteristics of an input signal. Shape, amplitude, and frequency of a waveform are represented on an oscilloscope.

output The signal taken out of any device; the name given to that jack out of which the signal is taken.

parameter A controllable and measurable quantity; in music, often used to describe the limitations of one element, i.e., the parameter of melody.

partial Any frequency component of a complex waveform, not necessarily related harmonically to the fundamental.

patch cord A wire with two plugs, one on each end, used with most synthesizers and studios; usually connected from the output of one device to the input of another.

pink noise A random signal (*see* white noise) in which the lower frequencies have been boosted and the higher frequencies attenuated.

pot *See* potentiometer.

potentiometer Often referred to as a "pot," this device is used to vary resistances or voltages in a circuit. (A loudness control is a common potentiometer.)

program The setup of an electronic device prior to its operation; a term applied usually to computers, but often to large synthesizers.

reverberation The rapid repetitions of an event as produced by the acoustic design of a room. These repetitions occur so quickly that they cannot be distinguished individually. Artificial reverberation may be produced by the manipulations of signals through an electronic device. (*See also* echo.)

Sel-sync The registered name of a device produced by Ampex Corp. for the selective synchronization of recordings. It allows the recording head to act as a playback head for those tracks not in the "record" mode. By canceling the time delay between the record and playback heads, the recording may be synchronized with the monitoring of the playbacks. A necessary device for multi-track recording.

signal The electrical analog of sound; that electrical current which finally operates the loudspeaker.

136

subaudio Frequencies generated below 30 Hz. In electronic music, these are usually employed for the purposes of modulation or as control voltages.

tape deck A reel-to-reel or cassette device which contains the recording, playback, and transport functions but is not equipped with amplifiers or speakers for monitoring.

tape loop A sound or combination of sounds that have been recorded on tape where the tape is arranged in such a way that the end of the event is spliced to the beginning to form a closed and repeating loop.

transients Frequency partials that are momentarily present in the attack of a tone.

tremelo Slight variations in loudness above and below a given dynamic level. The electronic analogy is *amplitude modulation.*

timbre Tone color. This is the aural representation of the relative amplitudes and frequencies of the transients, overtones, and partials of any complex waveform.

variable speed unit A device used to control and vary the speed of a tape recorder's capstan motor. On professional tape recorders, these motors are synchronized to the frequency of the AC current (60 Hz. in the United States). The variable-speed unit provides an oscillator that can be varied from 30 to 80 Hz., and an amplifier to boost the voltage produced by the oscillator to 117 V. This is then used to drive the tape recorder motor.

vibrato Slight vibrations of pitch above and below a particular note. Vibrato is employed by traditional instruments and voices to add a quality of "warmth." The electronic analogy is *frequency modulation.*

voltage control A method of controlling amplifiers, generators, and filters with small amounts of DC voltages applied to "control inputs." This is used in all synthesizers and allows for numerous such devices as keyboards, linear controllers, foot pedals, and sequencers to be used to control the various parameters.

white noise A signal that contains a continually random sampling of all frequencies and amplitudes within the audio range.

INDEX

acoustics, 59-62
aleatory, 12-15
amplifiers 68-70
analog devices, 73, 74, 108
Antheil, George, 8
Arel, Bulent, 13
ARP Synthesizers, 31, 76, 82, 93, 112
art trouvé, 9, 24
Audio Engineering Society, The, 31
audio frequency, 64

Babbitt, Milton, 15
Beatles, the, 16
Bell Telephone Laboratories, 33
Berg, Alban, 4
Berio, Luciano, 16
binary, 28, 109, 110
bruitism, 8, 25
Buchla, Donald, 31
Buchla Synthesizers, 31, 76, 93, 112

Cage, John, 13-15, 23, 24, 26
Cahill, Thaddeus, 20-21
Cologne Electronic Music Studio, 26, 27
Columbia University, 27
  (Electronic Music Studio, 28, 29)
computer, 32, 33, 34
control voltage, 32, 65, 73-75, 76, 101, 103, 107, 108, 111
  to amplifiers, 80-83, 103
  to oscillators, 75, 106
  to filters, 95, 106, 125

Corea, Chick, 16
Cowell, Henry, 22
Cunningham, Merce, 13

dadaism, 7-9, 25
Davidowsky, Mario, 16
Debussy, Claude, 2, 3-4
digital sequencers, 108-112
digital-to-analog converter, 33
Duchamp, Marcel, 24

echo loop, 50, 51, 130
echo, tape head, 51, 62, 118
Eimert, Herbert, 26
Electrocomp (EML) Synthesizers, 31, 32, 76, 92
Emerson, Keith, 16
envelope, 81, 82, 122, 124, 129
envelope generators, 81, 82, 95, 107, 129
Etherophone, 21

feedback, 51, 52
filters, 89-94, 97, 99
Foss, Lukas, 13, 15
frequency response curve, 55, 95

Hammond, Laurens, 22
Hammond organ, 22, 23
Henry, Pierre, 24-25
Hertz, Heinrich, 64
Hiller, Lejaren, 32
Hofstra University, 29, 30, 35
hydraulis, 19

I Ching, 12
Illinois, University of, 32
impedance, 56, 60
impressionism, 2, 3-4

LeCain, Hugh, 27, 28
Leuning, Otto, 27
loudspeakers, 63-64

Matthews, Max, 33
microphones, 55-56
modulation
  of frequency, 77-79, 128, 129
  of amplitude, 83-85, 101-102
  of filters, 95
  ring modulation, 103, 112
Moog, Robert A., 13, 21, 22, 30, 31
Moog Synthesizers, 31, 35, 73, 93, 98, 101, 112, 119, 120, 127, 128
Museum of Modern Art, 27
musique concrète, 9, 24-26, 29, 96, 115, 119, 120

New York Electric Music Company, 20, 21
Novachord, 23

Oberheim Synthesizers, 109
Ondes Martenot, 23
oscillators, 20, 21, 64, 74-75, 79, 96, 120, 121, 123
oscilloscope, 96, 97

panharmonicum, 19
panning, 54
patch panel (set-up of), 53-54
program equalizers, 94-95

Radio Corporation of America, 15, 21, 23
  (RCA Mark II Synthesizer, 28, 29)
Radiodiffusion-Television Française 25

random signals, 96-98
  (random signal generators, 97)
regeneration, 96
reverberation, 62, 98, 99
Rhea, T. L., 22
Roland Synthesizers, 31, 79, 82, 92, 104, 112, 126

sample-and-hold, 103-105
Satie, Eric, 8
Schaeffer, Pierre, 24-25
Schoenberg, Arnold, 4-7
Scott, Raymond, 27, 28
Seaman, Norman, 11, 12
Seley, Jason, 29, 30
sequencers, 105-112
serialism, 4-7
signal-to-noise ratio, 48-50
Solovox, 23
sound-on-sound, 46-49, 118
spectrum, harmonic, 20, 87, 89
Stockhausen, Karlheinz, 25, 26
Stravinsky, 9
Sobotnik, Morton, 31
Switched on Bach, 32
SYNTHI Synthesizers, 31, 77, 105, 109, 110, 111, 112

tape loop, 45-46, 117
tape, magnetic recording, 38-41
tape speed, 42-43, 115, 116
Telharmonium, 20-21, 22
Theremin, Leon, 21-22
  (the instrument, 21-22, 30, 37)
Thereminovox, 21
Toronto, University of, 27

Ussachevsky, Vladimir, 27
Varèse, Edgard, 10-12, 22, 62
VU meter, 49, 50

waveforms, 33, 64-68, 78, 84, 87-89, 96, 104, 121
Webern, Anton, 4, 10
white noise, 97

Zappa, Frank, 10